Improving Teaching Effectiveness

VARIATION IN IMPROVEMENT AMONG SCHOOLS *in the* INTENSIVE PARTNERSHIPS *for* EFFECTIVE TEACHING

ALICE HUGUET, DEBORAH J. HOLTZMAN, ABBY ROBYN, ELIZABETH D. STEINER, IVY TODD, LINDA CHOI, MATTHEW D. BAIRD, ITALO A. GUTIERREZ, MICHAEL S. GARET, BRIAN M. STECHER, JOHN ENGBERG

Sponsored by the Bill & Melinda Gates Foundation

For more information on this publication, visit www.rand.org/t/RRA124-1

Library of Congress Cataloging-in-Publication Data is available for this publication.
ISBN: 978-1-9774-0369-8

Published (2020) by the RAND Corporation
RAND® is a registered trademark.

The RAND Corporation is a research organization that develops solutions to public policy challenges to help make communities throughout the world safer and more secure, healthier and more prosperous. RAND is nonprofit, nonpartisan, and committed to the public interest.

RAND's publications do not necessarily reflect the opinions of its research clients and sponsors.

Support RAND
Make a tax-deductible charitable contribution at
www.rand.org/giving/contribute

www.rand.org

Preface

From 2009–2010 to 2015–2016, the RAND Corporation and the American Institutes for Research (AIR) conducted an evaluation of the Bill & Melinda Gates Foundation's Intensive Partnerships for Effective Teaching (IP). As a result of that effort, the RAND-AIR team produced the following final report, three interim reports, and two journal articles:[1]

- Brian M. Stecher, Deborah J. Holtzman, Michael S. Garet, Laura S. Hamilton, John Engberg, Elizabeth D. Steiner, Abby Robyn, Matthew D. Baird, Italo A. Gutierrez, Evan D. Peet, Iliana Brodziak de los Reyes, Kaitlin Fronberg, Gabriel Weinberger, Gerald Paul Hunter, and Jay Chambers, *Improving Teaching Effectiveness: Final Report—The Intensive Partnerships for Effective Teaching Through 2015–2016*, Santa Monica, Calif.: RAND Corporation, RR-2242-BMGF, 2018
- Brian M. Stecher, Michael S. Garet, Laura S. Hamilton, Elizabeth D. Steiner, Abby Robyn, Jeffrey Poirier, Deborah Holtzman, Eleanor S. Fulbeck, Jay Chambers, and Iliana Brodziak de los Reyes, *Improving Teaching Effectiveness: Implementation—The Intensive Partnerships for Effective Teaching Through 2013–2014*, Santa Monica, Calif.: RAND Corporation, RR-1295-BMGF, 2016
- Matthew D. Baird, John Engberg, Gerald Paul Hunter, and Benjamin Master, *Improving Teaching Effectiveness: Access to Effec-*

---

[1] We also prepared a series of internal reports for the foundation and the sites.

tive Teaching—The Intensive Partnerships for Effective Teaching Through 2013–2014, Santa Monica, Calif.: RAND Corporation, RR-1295/4-BMGF, 2016

- Italo A. Gutierrez, Gabriel Weinberger, and John Engberg, *Improving Teaching Effectiveness: Impact on Student Outcomes— The Intensive Partnerships for Effective Teaching Through 2013– 2014*, Santa Monica, Calif.: RAND Corporation, RR-1295/3-1-BMGF, 2016
- Gema Zamarro, John Engberg, Juan Esteban Saavedra, and Jennifer Steele, "Disentangling Disadvantage: Can We Distinguish Good Teaching from Classroom Composition?" *Journal of Research on Educational Effectiveness*, Vol. 8, No. 1, 2015, pp. 84–111
- Brian Stecher, Mike Garet, Deborah Holtzman, and Laura Hamilton, "Implementing Measures of Teacher Effectiveness," *Phi Delta Kappan*, Vol. 94, No. 3, November 2012, pp. 39–43.

After the formal end of the initiative, the foundation wanted to know whether there were some schools in which the initiative was more successful, and if so, what conditions were correlated with better school-level outcomes; that is the focus of this report. This report should be of interest to the foundation staff and other members of the K–12 education reform community who are interested in a deeper look at the IP initiative.

This research was conducted by RAND Education and Labor, a division of the RAND Corporation that conducts research on early childhood through postsecondary education programs, workforce development, and programs and policies affecting workers, entrepreneurship, and financial literacy and decisionmaking.

This research also was conducted by AIR. Established in 1946, AIR is an independent, nonpartisan, not-for-profit organization that conducts behavioral and social science research on important social issues and delivers technical assistance in the areas of education, health, and workforce productivity.

More information about AIR can be found at www.air.org.

This report is based on research funded by the Bill & Melinda Gates Foundation. The findings and conclusions we present are those of the authors and do not necessarily reflect positions or policies of the Bill & Melinda Gates Foundation. For more information, please visit www.gatesfoundation.org.

More information about RAND can be found at www.rand.org. Questions about this report should be directed to engberg@rand.org, and questions about RAND Education and Labor should be directed to educationandlabor@rand.org.

Contents

Figures

Tables

Summary

In the 2009–2010 school year, the Bill & Melinda Gates Foundation launched the Intensive Partnerships for Effective Teaching (IP) initiative to improve achievement among low-income minority (LIM) students. The initiative established and provided ongoing support for several human capital reforms that were theorized to result in improved teaching effectiveness (TE) areas, such as teacher workforce conditions (e.g., hiring, retention, dismissal), teacher-evaluation policies, individualized professional development (PD), strategic compensation, and career ladders. The IP theory of action posited that implementation of these levers would improve TE over time and offer LIM students more access to effective teachers, which would in turn improve student achievement and graduation rates. Three public school districts and four charter management organizations (CMOs) participated in the initiative; throughout this report, we refer to these districts and CMOs as *sites*.[1] The Gates Foundation awarded $290,000,000 to these sites and provided ongoing technical assistance to help them implement the initiative.

The RAND Corporation and the American Institutes for Research evaluated the implementation of the IP initiative and its impact on student outcomes. We studied the initiative throughout its six years of implementation, interviewing central office administrators, school leaders, and teachers; surveying school leaders and teachers; and collecting staff administrative records, student administrative

---

[1]   That is, where we use the word *site*, we are referring to a district or a CMO. We are *not* referring to an individual school.

records, student achievement data, fiscal records, and other pertinent implementation information. In addition, we selected two to seven case-study schools in each site, interviewing school leaders and teachers annually and conducting site visits biennially. We issued a final report in 2018 that detailed our findings through the end of the initiative in 2016 (Stecher et al., 2018). We found that the initiative was not successful in meeting its goals. Student achievement, access to effective teachers, and dropout rates were not substantially better in the IP sites than in similar sites that did not participate in the initiative.

The Gates Foundation, along with the RAND and AIR researchers, speculated that perhaps there were lessons to be learned from variation among schools within the IP sites because some schools had improved more than others. To investigate the factors that might be associated with positive student outcomes at the school level, we took two complementary approaches: We conducted a qualitative study and a survey study. For the qualitative study, we selected pairs of schools from each of four IP sites—Hillsborough County Public Schools (HCPS) in Florida, Pittsburgh Public Schools (PPS) in Pennsylvania, Shelby County Schools (SCS) in Tennessee, and Aspire Public Schools in California—that were similar in terms of achievement, teacher value added, and student demographics at the beginning of the initiative but showed differing levels of improvement *during* the initiative. Improvement was measured by growth in test scores and growth in teacher value added. We visited the school pairs in spring 2018, eliciting teacher and principal perspectives on several factors that were potentially relevant to their schools' improvement. The research staff who collected and analyzed the qualitative data remained blind to which schools were in the improving and nonimproving groups until the final stages of analysis. In the survey study, we used teacher surveys that were administered in the spring of each year from 2013 through 2016 to look for relationships between staff beliefs and school-level improvement over the course of the IP initiative. In both studies, we looked for indications of dissimilarities between the improving and nonimproving schools. These two studies use different samples, use different methods, and address somewhat different questions about the correlates of positive student outcomes. Therefore, each produces valuable insights, leading to a more nuanced understanding than either could on its own.

The Qualitative Study

Our team first identified 11 pairs of IP schools in the four sites that were similar at baseline but experienced different levels of improvement during the initiative. Within each pair, the improving school was among the highest performing in its site in improvements in achievement levels, access to effective teachers, and value added. Each non-improving school exhibited changes near the site average in these categories.

Interviews were our primary source of data in the qualitative study. Our interview protocols were informed by grounded theory and included broad questions designed to enable unexpected themes to emerge based on participant responses. We also included questions designed to elicit interviewees' perspectives on the initiative itself. At each selected school, we interviewed four or five teachers and one or more school leaders (i.e., principal or assistant principal) who worked at the school during the focal period of the initiative. The focal period varied for each site based on their rollout of the initiative; in HCPS and PPS, the baseline period ended in spring 2010, and the mature-implementation period ended in spring 2016; for SCS, the periods ended in 2011 and 2015, respectively; and for Aspire, they ended in 2010 and 2015, respectively. We conducted a total of 120 interviews across the four sites. All interviews were recorded, and we had the audio transcribed.

To minimize bias, researchers working on the qualitative portion of this study remained blind to schools' improvement status for the majority of the analysis. Once coding and initial analyses were complete, schools' identities as improvers or nonimprovers during the focal period were revealed, and we identified patterns across all 22 participating schools (11 pairs) regardless of the site to which they belonged. We also looked *within* each site to identify similarities and differences between the schools that did and did not improve.

Qualitative Study Findings

Associations emerged between a variety of interview themes and school improvement during the focal period. The themes associated with improvement included aspects of principal leadership, perceptions of staff cohesion, and factors outside the schools' control that interviewees felt influenced their success. There are various ways in which the categories interacted with one another; for instance, staff cohesion was often discussed in conjunction with leadership. Therefore, we suggest interpreting these factors as interreliant rather than independent.

Interviewees reported that principals engaged in specific behaviors that were associated with school improvement. Two leadership behaviors were notably more prominent in improving schools than in their paired counterparts: Principals reportedly facilitated collaboration and learning among staff members and gave teachers decision-making power in the form of autonomy in their classrooms and input into school decisions.

Interviewee perceptions of cohesiveness among school staff also appeared to be related to school improvement. Interviewees at improving schools more often reported broad support for a common mission than their counterparts at nonimproving schools. Also, in nonimproving schools, it was more common for interviewees to discuss divisiveness between groups of staff members than it was in improving schools. Interviewees linked both of these factors to the cohesiveness of school staff but tended to discuss them in relationship to leadership behaviors.

Finally, three factors that were perceived to be beyond schools' control were mentioned more frequently in nonimproving schools than in improving schools: (1) interviewees reported that competing schools siphoned off strong students; (2) interviewees suggested that their students' potential for achievement was constrained by demographic shifts in their schools; and (3) interviewees had negative reactions to student discipline policies during the focal period. Interviewees at nonimproving schools appeared to believe that these factors had at least as much of an effect on student learning as anything within their control as educators. Our data do not confirm that demographic shifts in schools were associated with nonimprovement. By design, our research team restricted the pool from which we drew our case-study schools to those without extreme demographic changes during the focal period. Therefore, these kinds of comments might not be reflective of actual demographic shifts; rather, they might reflect interviewees' perceptions or beliefs.

In the qualitative study, interviewee reports regarding the actual levers of the IP initiative—teacher-evaluation processes, staffing policies, PD practices, career ladders, and compensation policies—did not emerge as associated with patterns in school improvement. We did not attempt to gauge fidelity of implementation but instead explored interviewees' recollections of how the levers worked, what effects they thought the levers had on their own practice, and how they and fellow staff felt about the levers at the time they were implemented.

When we look at the qualitative findings collectively, interviewees at improving schools were more likely to report feeling that they had control over their classrooms and school experiences than those at nonimproving schools. For instance, some felt that they were treated as experts in their practice or that they were able to make their own school and classroom decisions. At nonimproving schools, interviewees were more likely to report ways that their students' or schools' achievement was outside their control and that such achievement was constrained in particular by the three external factors we noted earlier.

The Survey Study

To complement the qualitative study, we also made use of teacher survey data that had been collected during the IP initiative. Specifically, we looked for relationships between staff beliefs and school-level improvement over the course of the initiative. These analyses used data from 377 schools in the four sites that were part of the variation study.

Our measures of staff beliefs were 12 multi-item survey scales, aggregated to the school level. Most of the scales related to teachers' attitudes and beliefs about the levers of the IP initiative (e.g., evaluation systems, PD, compensation reform), while a few focused on more-general constructs, such as district support and school environment (e.g., supportive climate and collaboration).

We then tested the association of each of these scale variables with school improvement, as operationalized by improvement in the teacher value-added modeling (VAM) measure. This was done separately by site and then combined using meta-analysis, allowing us to examine the relationships overall and whether they varied across sites. This measure of improvement is a component of that used by the qualitative study, which also incorporated the increase in average test scores.

Survey Study Findings

We found that, combined across all four sites, the following seven survey scales were significantly related to school improvement:

- supportive district climate
- supportive and respectful school environment
- impetus for and impact of PD
- alignment and relevance of PD
- support for the evaluation system
- validity of the student achievement component of the evaluation system
- fairness of compensation.

None of these seven scales had significant variation across sites in its relationship with school average VAM scores. However, three others showed significant variation across sites. One was "rapport among teachers," for which the effect was larger and more positive in the three districts than in Aspire. The other two were "expectations for students" and "validity of the student input component of the evaluation system." For each of these two scales, SCS's effect was larger and more positive than the effect in the other three sites.

Limitations

Although the associations found by the studies are consistent with a causal relationship in which leadership and staff behaviors and perspectives had an impact on student learning, our studies were not designed to support causal inferences. In this report, we describe more-detailed limitations of the qualitative and survey studies.

Conclusion

Using both studies, we found that schools were more likely to improve where certain leadership behaviors were reported, such as principals fostering collaborative environments or offering opportunities for teachers to take part in decisionmaking. The qualitative study also found that schools were more likely to improve where interviewees reported a sense of unity among staff and schools were less likely to improve where interviewees reported that factors outside their schools' control influenced success. The qualitative study did not find a relationship between interviewee perspectives regarding features of the IP initiative and school improvement, but the survey study found that perceptions of some elements of the IP initiative were associated with improvement. We do not believe that one study is more reliable than the other; the studies are distinct enough to offer different perspectives.

The two studies used different methods, but to the extent that they explored similar factors or conditions, one might expect them to yield similar findings—and in some respects, they did. But the qualitative study and the survey study were designed and conducted at different times and for different purposes. In this report, we discuss possible explanations for differences between the qualitative and survey findings and provide some suggestions for others doing similar research in the future.

Acknowledgments

This research builds on the work of many people who contributed to the original Intensive Partnerships for Effective Teaching (IP) initiative and study (Stecher et al., 2018). Although we do not list all of their names here, this study could not have been undertaken without the care they showed in designing, implementing, measuring, and evaluating that mammoth effort in reforming the way that teachers are evaluated, supported, and compensated.

For the present study of variation among schools in the IP initiative, we are particularly grateful to leaders and staff of Hillsborough County Public Schools (HCPS), Pittsburgh Public Schools (PPS), Shelby County Schools (SCS), and Aspire Public Schools who continued to work with us after the initial IP evaluation period so that additional lessons could be learned from that experience. We appreciate the efforts of central-office staff members who provided information about each site's implementation efforts, helped us coordinate our communication with staff, facilitated our access to site data, and reviewed our tables and charts for accuracy. These staff members include Jessica Doherty, Julie McLeod, and Marie Whelan of HCPS; Tara Tucci, Ted Dwyer, and Deb Friss of PPS; Anasa Franklin and Jessica Lotz of SCS; and James Gallagher and Ben Crosby of Aspire. We also want to extend our genuine thanks to the administrators and teachers in the participating schools who were generous in sharing their experiences with our team.

We also appreciate the willingness of staff at the Bill & Melinda Gates Foundation to support this additional analysis of the IP initiative and engage with us throughout; we are especially grateful to our program officers, Eli Pristoop, Alex Resch, and Andrew Sokatch, for their advice and responsiveness throughout the project. The findings and conclusions contained within this report are those of the authors and do not necessarily reflect the positions or policies of the Bill & Melinda Gates Foundation.

We thank Fatih Unlu and John Pane of RAND and Douglas Lee Lauen of the University of North Carolina–Chapel Hill for reviewing the report and providing constructive feedback. Finally, we acknowledge other members of the RAND team, including Jan M. Hanley, Gerald Hunter, Stephanie Lonsinger, and Stephanie Williamson, and members of the American Institutes for Research team, including Candace Hester and Charlotte Chen.

Abbreviations

AIR	American Institutes for Research
ASD	Achievement School District
CI	confidence interval
CMO	charter management organization
ELA	English language arts
ELL	English language learner
HCPS	Hillsborough County Public Schools
ICC	intracluster correlation coefficient
IP	Intensive Partnerships for Effective Teaching
LIM	low-income minority
OLS	ordinary least squares
PD	professional development
PPS	Pittsburgh Public Schools
SCS	Shelby County Schools
TE	teaching effectiveness
VAM	value-added modeling

CHAPTER ONE

Introduction

The Intensive Partnerships for Effective Teaching Initiative and Evaluation

In the 2009–2010 school year, the Bill & Melinda Gates Foundation launched the Intensive Partnerships for Effective Teaching (IP) initiative to improve achievement among low-income minority (LIM) students by implementing several human capital reforms that were theorized to result in improved teaching effectiveness (TE). Participating sites were required to implement an evaluation system based on a rigorous measure of TE that included a measure of student achievement growth, structured observations of teaching practice, and other measures that varied by site. The TE measure was to be used to inform hiring, placement, retention, and dismissal decisions; professional development (PD) policies to support improved teacher practices; teacher compensation policies; and the development of teacher career ladders. The IP theory of action posited that implementation of these levers would improve TE over time and offer LIM students more access to effective teachers, which would in turn improve student achievement and graduation rates. The five levers that the IP initiative focused on were teacher workforce conditions (e.g., hiring, retention, dismissal), teacher-evaluation policies, individualized PD, strategic compensation, and career ladders.

Three public school districts and four charter management organizations (CMOs) participated in the initiative.[1] Throughout this report, we refer to these districts and CMOs as *sites*.[2] The Gates Foundation initially planned to award $290,000,000 to these seven sites (to be distributed roughly in proportion to student enrollment); the amount was later amended to be $250,000,000, of which approximately $240,000,000 had been spent through the 2015–2016 school year (Garet et al., 2019). The foundation also provided ongoing technical assistance to the sites to help them implement the initiative.

The foundation contracted with the RAND Corporation and the American Institutes for Research (AIR) to evaluate the implementation of the IP initiative and its impact on student outcomes. We studied the initiative throughout its six years of implementation, interviewing central office administrators, school leaders, and teachers; surveying school leaders and teachers; and collecting staff administrative records, student achievement data, fiscal records, and other pertinent implementation information. In addition, we selected two to seven case-study schools in each site, interviewing school leaders and teachers annually and visiting biennially.[3]

We issued a final report in 2018 that detailed our findings through the end of the initiative in 2016 (see Stecher et al., 2018). We found that all of the sites implemented an evaluation system that included both student achievement and structured observational measures of TE, and that these measures played a role in some human resource decisions.

---

[1]   The three school districts were Hillsborough County Public Schools (HCPS) in Tampa, Florida; Pittsburgh Public Schools (PPS) in Pittsburgh, Pennsylvania; and Shelby County Schools (SCS; formerly Memphis City Schools) in Memphis, Tennessee. The four CMOs, which were initially organized as a consortium called The College Ready Promise, were Alliance College-Ready Public Schools, Aspire Public Schools, Green Dot Public Schools, and Partnership to Uplift Communities Schools. All four are based in California.

[2]   That is, where we use the word *site*, we are referring to a district or a CMO. We are *not* referring to an individual school.

[3]   We visited all of the case-study schools in 2010–2011; we then divided the sample in half and visited the schools in each half every other year. In each school's "off" year, we interviewed the school leader and several teachers by telephone. These case-study schools were not the same as those discussed in Chapter Two of this report.

However, the initiative was not successful in meeting its goals. Student achievement, access to effective teachers, and dropout rates were not substantially better in the IP sites than in similar sites that did not participate in the initiative. There are several possible explanations for these results, including a lack of complete implementation of key policies and practices (such as limited individualization of PD to address teacher needs); a flawed theory of action; challenges related to linking teacher retention, dismissal, and compensation to measures of TE; the impact of such external factors as changes in state policies; and insufficient time for the initiative to show positive outcomes.

Purpose of This Study

The Gates Foundation and the RAND-AIR study team speculated that perhaps there were lessons to be learned from variation among schools within the IP sites because, undoubtedly, some schools had improved more than others during the initiative. In response, the foundation funded a supplemental qualitative study of selected schools that were initially similar in student composition and performance but showed different levels of improvement during the initiative. The qualitative analyses were complemented by additional analyses of the teacher survey responses collected during the initiative.

We took two complementary approaches to examine the factors that might be associated with positive student outcomes at the school level. These two studies use different samples, use different methods, and address somewhat different questions about the correlates of positive student outcomes. Therefore, each produces valuable insights, leading to a more nuanced understanding than either could on its own.

First, we identified pairs of schools in each of the three districts and in Aspire—the four sites large enough to support this analysis—that were similar at baseline in terms of average achievement, average teacher value added,[4] and percentage of LIM students, but that

---

[4]   *Teacher value added* is an estimate of an individual teacher's contribution to student learning based on the growth of assessment test scores for students in the teacher's classes.

showed differing levels of improvement in achievement level and value added during the initiative (while not showing extreme changes in demographics). In other words, one school in each pair showed markedly greater improvement in student achievement than the other. (See Appendix A for a description of the school selection process.) We examined two to three pairs of schools in each of the four IP sites in this analysis for a total of 11 schools with improved outcomes matched with 11 schools whose outcomes had not improved during the period each site implemented the IP initiative (typically from 2011 to 2016). We visited these schools in spring 2018 and talked with school leaders and teachers to elicit their perspectives on several factors that possibly were relevant to their improvement status, including their perspectives on the implementation of the initiative and the organizational and environmental context of the schools during the focal period.[5] The research staff who conducted these interviews remained blind to which schools were in the group with greater improvement and which schools were in the comparison group.

Our second approach to studying variation was based on the surveys that had been conducted as part of the original IP evaluation, especially the teacher surveys that were administered in the spring of each year from 2013 through 2016. Because we had surveyed teachers in every school in each of the IP sites in multiple years, we had a comprehensive set of data that we thought might complement the qualitative study. At the school level, we examined whether each of 12 scales based on the teacher survey data was associated with improvement in school-level achievement outcomes. Eight of the 12 scales were related to the IP levers; the other four were related to district and school context.

---

[5]   For HCPS and PPS, the focal period was from 2010–2011 to 2015–2016; for SCS, it was from 2011–2012 to 2014–2015; and for Aspire, it was from 2009–2010 to 2015–2016. We describe the parameters for the focal periods, including the availability of data, in Chapter Two of this report.

Organization of This Report

In Chapter Two, we describe our qualitative study of variation between improving and nonimproving schools. In Chapter Three, we present the results of our survey analyses, which examined similar relationships. To better understand the similarities and differences between the results from the qualitative study and the survey study, we present a comparison and discussion of the findings from these two complementary studies and some concluding comments in Chapter Four. In Appendixes A and B, we provide more detail on our methods for the qualitative study and the survey study, respectively.

CHAPTER TWO

Qualitative Study

Many studies of the factors leading to school improvement examine only schools identified as effective.[1] In designing our study, we were wary of such an approach because it can lead to misleading inferences. Without studying schools that are *not* considered to be effective (or improving), one cannot know whether the factors that seem to be associated with the successful schools also might be present in the unsuccessful schools. Moreover, there could be lessons to be learned about why some schools are *not* successful, and these lessons most likely can come only from such schools. Thus, we decided to study both improving and nonimproving schools. A further benefit of this approach is that it allowed for our qualitative data collectors and analysts to be "blind" to the groups to which any given school belongs, thereby reducing the likelihood that the identification of factors associated with improvement might stem from researcher bias, conscious or unconscious.

In this chapter, we describe our qualitative study methods and results. We begin with a review of our study methods, including the selection of study schools and our choice of interview subjects, interview methods, and coding and analysis methods. More detail is provided on each of these items in Appendix A. We then describe our qualitative findings.

---

[1] A particular line of research focuses on schools "beating the odds"; that is, schools that have performed better than statistically predicted based on demographic composition. See, for example, Langer, 2001, and Ascher and Maguire, 2007.

Methods

In this section, we describe the qualitative case-study approach we took to identifying factors that differentiated schools that improved from schools that did not, including the selection of schools and participants, design of our interview protocol, analyses of interview transcripts, and identification of factors associated with improvement. Finally, we discuss some of the limitations of the approach we applied.

School Selection

By using a case-study approach to examine schools that improved and similar schools that did not, we aimed to better understand conditions associated with improvement. Our first task was to identify pairs of schools in each of four IP sites—HCPS in Florida, PPS in Pennsylvania, SCS in Tennessee, and Aspire Public Schools in California—that were similar at baseline but that subsequently diverged in their trajectories during the years of the IP initiative. In this section, we provide a summary of the process we used to identify the schools. A detailed description of this selection process is presented in Appendix A.

We used information for three years prior to IP implementation to develop baseline measures and for three years toward the end of the initiative grant period as the basis for mature-implementation measures, reflecting a point by which we expected that the initiative would have produced change. Because of data availability, the years used to construct these measures differed slightly among the sites. For HCPS and PPS, the baseline period ended in spring 2010, and the mature-implementation period ended in spring 2016; for SCS, the periods ended in 2011 and 2015, respectively; and for Aspire, the periods ended in 2010 and 2015, respectively. For the purposes of the qualitative study, we referred to the first year following the baseline period through the final year of the mature-implementation period (e.g., in HCPS, the 2010–2011 school year through the 2015–2016 school year) as the *focal period*: that is, the period of implementation during which the improvement could have occurred and to which we should look to identify factors that could have contributed to the improvement (or the lack thereof).

To select the schools, we began with the set of all schools in the four sites for which we could calculate a school-level measure of value added. Value added is calculated on the basis of student test score growth and requires, at a minimum, scores from the previous year and the current year for each student. State assessments are given in grades 3 through 8, so this restricted our sample to schools that offered some subset of grades 4 through 8. We used all teachers for whom we could calculate either an English language arts (ELA) or mathematics value added; for those who taught both subjects, we took the average. The school's value added is the precision-weighted average of the value-added estimates of teachers in the school.

We then restricted the pool of potential case-study sites to schools that had not dramatically changed in student demographic composition from baseline (see Appendix A for further detail). That is, we limited our pool to schools without extreme changes in the distribution of student race/ethnicity and the percentage of English language learner (ELL), gifted (where available), and economically disadvantaged students between the baseline and mature-implementation periods.

The improving case-study schools were selected by finding several schools from each site that had improved most between the site's baseline and mature-implementation years, as measured by growth in test scores and growth in average teacher value added. For each improving school, we found a nonimproving school that matched it on baseline measures of average value added, average test scores, percentage of LIM students, and grade configuration.

Ultimately, we selected 11 pairs of schools: three pairs (six schools) each in HCPS, SCS, and Aspire, and two pairs (four schools) in PPS. We contacted central office administrators at each of the four sites and asked permission to conduct interviews in these pairs of schools without revealing which were improving schools and which were nonimproving schools. In this process, we had to adjust our selection at some points because of school nonresponse, and in one site because of district concerns. We had limited options available in PPS; therefore, one of the two pairs we used had little contrast in growth between the improving and the nonimproving school.

In sum, when we refer to a school as an *improving* school, we mean a school that was among the highest in its site in the improvement of both achievement levels and value added during the focal period and that did not experience an extreme change in student demographics. Its paired *nonimproving* school is one that was similar at baseline on achievement, value added, and percentage of LIM students to one of the improvers in the same site, but with a change in achievement and value added that was near the site average and also was without an extreme change in demographics. Therefore, improvement is a relative concept within each site—a school we call *nonimproving* might have improved in an absolute sense, but not relative to the site average. We use relative improvement to avoid concerns about the equivalence of test scales over time.

Participant Selection

We planned to interview five teachers and one or more school leaders at each of the 22 selected schools. To select the teachers, we used staff rosters and website listings to identify individuals who had taught at the school during the focal period and who were currently teaching at the school.[2] Our goal was to select teachers who had been at the school since the beginning of the focal period, but there were not always five such teachers, so we also considered teachers who arrived during the focal period. When there were more than five teachers who fit this criteria, we selected based on the variety of grades and subjects taught. We also requested an interview with the current principal at each school, regardless of whether they were present during the focal period. In cases where the current principal arrived at the school after the focal period, we contacted a past principal to request an interview. If an assistant principal from the focal period remained on staff, we interviewed them as well.

---

2   In one school, only one teacher who had been there during the focal period was still at that school at the time of our interviews. We located some of the teachers and the principal at a new school and interviewed them there in reference to the selected school.

Protocol Development

The IP evaluation previously explored implementation of the five major levers emphasized by the initiative: teacher-evaluation processes, staffing policies, PD practices, career ladders for teachers, and compensation policies. Rather than trying to isolate these levers in our qualitative inquiry, we asked open-ended questions, seeking to understand how dimensions of the school organizations and their environmental contexts were associated with school improvement status, if at all. We probed on topics specified in advance but also asked broad questions to elicit responses regarding a wide variety of unanticipated issues that interviewees believed were prominent in their schools. We developed semistructured interview protocols that asked the same questions in each school but allowed respondents to elaborate or offer unsolicited input. This approach allowed us to investigate participant perspectives on dimensions of the initiative itself, along with factors exogenous to the initiative that were deemed important by interviewees. See Appendix A for details regarding how we developed protocols and for the full teacher and principal protocols.

Data Collection

We conducted the interviews in spring 2018. In Table 2.1, we show the number of teachers and administrators we interviewed in each of the four sites and overall. Two team members visited each case-study school for one day and conducted 30- to 60-minute interviews with the selected staff members. We conducted phone interviews with principals who had been employed at case-study schools during the focal period but who no longer worked at the specific school. Team members took notes and recorded audio during the interviews. We had the audio professionally transcribed.

A key strength of the study design was that the interviewers remained blind to the improvement statuses of the schools. This enabled them to avoid bias in asking the interview questions and in

Table 2.1
Interviews Conducted, by Site

Site	Teachers	Administrators[a]	Total
HCPS (6 schools)	26	8	34
PPS (4 schools)	18	4	22
SCS (6 schools)	26	6	32
Aspire (6 schools)	24	8	32
Total	94	26	120

[a] Administrators were primarily principals, although in some cases, we interviewed a current principal who was an assistant principal during the focal period.

interpreting responses. Blindness to condition continued until well into the analysis process.[3]

Coding and Analysis

We coded the interview transcripts iteratively using the qualitative analysis software Dedoose, applying deductive and inductive codes. We based deductive codes on the interview protocol; these included dimensions of the school organization, the district and environment, initiative levers, and codes that were used to identify strengths and challenges noted by interviewees (see Appendix A for the complete protocols). We coded not only for the topic of an excerpt's content but also for the time frame: for instance, whether the reference was to the focal period, current period, both, or unclear. We then drew from excerpts that we had confirmed were referring to the focal period. Inductive codes were created when we identified unanticipated themes that emerged across multiple schools. The inductive codes were developed collaboratively during regular calibration conversations among coders.

We used a matrix-based approach to analyze the coded data and look for patterns and relationships. We created a matrix with each row

[3] After our coding was complete, we checked the effectiveness of our efforts to keep the coders blind to the actual improver status of the schools in the sample. We asked the coders to guess whether each school was an improver or a nonimprover. The guesses were 60-percent accurate. Although the guesses were better than chance, we think this supports the claim that coders were generally not aware of each school's status while they were coding the interviews.

representing a case-study school and each column representing a factor that was potentially relevant to school improvement status. We initially populated each cell with a summary of a particular factor at a specific school (e.g., staff buy-in to the initiative at a school). Then we assigned values to each cell based on the topic of the column to describe the implementation status of each factor. For instance, for cells related to perceptions of school buy-in during the focal period, we assigned the value "bought in," "not bought in," "mixed," or "insufficient information" based on the broader collection of data we had summarized. We color-coded cells to more easily identify patterns. (We describe the analysis process in more detail in Appendix A.) We wrote memos summarizing themes as they emerged and discussed them among our team. To minimize bias, coders remained blind to schools' improvement status during this phase of the analysis.

Revealing the Improvement Statuses of Schools

Once the coding and initial matrix analyses were complete, schools' identities as improvers or nonimprovers during the focal period were revealed to some members of the qualitative team; others remained blind to improver status so that they could be called on to conduct unbiased follow-up analyses. Those who learned the schools' statuses added a column for improvement status to the existing matrix. We identified patterns in improvers and nonimprovers across all 22 participating schools, regardless of the site to which they belonged. We also looked *within* each site in the matrix to identify similarities and differences between the schools that did and did not improve. Although the matrix approach helped us break complex dimensions of schools and their environments into discrete factors for analysis, it was by considering each factor in relationship to the others and assessing the evidence holistically that we were able to discern patterns. For instance, when we analyzed the degree of staff cohesion reported in SCS, we noted that interviewees' comments often were linked to leadership. Our process addressed the relationship between these factors rather than treating staff cohesion and leadership as two completely independent factors. We held regular conversations as a team to discuss our developing interpretation of these patterns and the relationship between these patterns and our broader understanding of the initiative. The qualitative findings described in this report are the result of these processes.

Limitations of the Case Study Data Collection and Analysis

Our findings cannot be used to draw causal conclusions about the relationship between identified factors and school performance; they represent only *associations* between particular factors and school improvement. Additionally, our case-study approach has at least three other key limitations related to the use of retrospective interviews, our interviewee sampling strategy, and the possibility of biased interpretations of the data.

Retrospective interviews rely on individual interviewees' memories, both real and constructed, and are therefore susceptible to inaccuracies and variation in interpretations. Interviewees' recollections might have been influenced by the present and by their own perceptions of whether their school had made improvements during or since the focal period. Other human factors, such as faulty memories, might have prevented salient details from emerging; for instance, it might not be realistic to expect teachers to recall details about the PD they received four years ago. The IP levers might not have been particularly salient to interviewees at the time of the initiative, and it is possible that they were even less so at the time of our interviews. We attempted to mitigate the problems of retrospective interviewing by mentioning—both early on in each interview and at intervals during the interviews—concrete reminders of the focal period, such as dates, names of site and school leaders at the time, and important events in the community. Our hope was that these reminders would jog interviewees' memories and increase the likelihood that they would accurately recall the period in which we were interested.

A second limitation concerns our sampling strategy. By design, the teachers we interviewed had all worked at their schools since the focal period and were still there at the time of data collection. We wanted to interview teachers who would remember their school during the focal period, but this strategy introduced bias into our sample because it excluded teachers who worked at the school during the focal period but had since left. These teachers might have had systematically different perspectives regarding the school during the focal period than those who remained employed at the school at the time of the interviews. We also did not restrict interview sampling to teachers in tested grades and subjects—that is, those who contributed most directly to school selection criteria.

Finally, although our team took measures to remain as impartial as possible and to reduce the risk of conscious and unconscious bias during data collection and analysis—including remaining blind to the improver or nonimprover status of each of the 22 schools in the study until the final phase of analysis—all data analysis involves some degree of subjective interpretation. As we analyzed our data, our team had to make decisions about what kinds of thresholds to set and when a particular school fell on one side of a threshold (e.g., the amount and type of interview information required to determine whether the initiative was messaged in a way that was constructive or nonconstructive at a school). We used consensus and discussion to remain as neutral as possible in making analytic decisions. Despite these limitations, we think this analysis sheds light on factors that could be associated with school improvement.

Results

Several associations emerged between interview themes and school improvement during the focal period. In this section, we describe relationships identified through comparison of the interviewees'—both administrators' and teachers'—responses from improving and nonimproving schools. It was never the case that a factor was described by respondents in *all* the improving schools across sites and in *none* of the nonimproving schools (or vice versa); however, there were many instances in which features appeared more frequently, or were described by interviewees as more impactful in one group of schools than the other. These features included aspects of principal leadership, perceptions of staff cohesion, and references to factors outside schools' control that interviewees felt influenced their school's success. In this section, we describe findings based on a pooled analysis across all 22 schools but also highlight when they appeared particularly salient in specific sites. Although we discuss each factor sequentially in this chapter, there are various ways in which they interact with one another; for instance, staff cohesion often was discussed in conjunction with conversations about leadership. Therefore, we suggest interpreting these factors as interreliant rather than independent. Finally, we outline some factors that we had expected to be associated with school improvement but were not.

Principal Leadership

Several aspects of leadership were associated with school improvement status. First, improving schools were more likely than nonimproving schools to have consistent leadership during the focal period: Of the seven schools with at least one administrator who remained on campus for the full duration of the focal period, five were improvers.[4] There also were specific behaviors that principals engaged in, as reported by interviewees, that were associated with school improvement. Two categories of leadership behaviors were notably more prominent in interviewee reports from improving schools: (1) that principals facilitated collaboration and learning among staff members and (2) that they were more likely to give teachers decisionmaking power—both autonomy in their classrooms and input into school decisions.

> ## Principals at improving schools facilitated collaboration among staff during the focal period.

Interviewees at improving schools were more likely than those at nonimproving schools to report that their school leaders encouraged and structured collaboration between—and learning among—school staff. There were six schools in our study in which multiple interviewees explicitly described their principals as facilitating teacher collaboration, and all six of these schools were improvers. There were five schools in which interviewees reported that they had no or minimal

---

[4]   This finding was derived from administrative data on the case-study schools, not from interview data.

interteacher collaboration during the focal period, and four of these five schools were nonimprovers.[5]

There were multiple ways in which interviewees discussed collaboration during the focal period. In some schools, encouraging collaboration meant structuring planning meetings for teachers; in others, it meant asking teachers with specific skills to provide PD to the rest of the staff. Teachers in some schools reported that their leaders imparted a general collaborative philosophy; for example, one interviewee at an improving school recollected that

> [There was a] sense of urgency that [the principal] gave us. It was contagious. It was a contagious spirit throughout the building, "Okay, let's do this, let's be intentional, let's be collaborative around everything that we're doing."

Most teachers at improving schools recalled collaboration in a positive light. They viewed opportunities for learning from their peers as an effective way to develop their practice. A teacher at another improving school told us that she was able to develop novel skills by participating in classroom walkthroughs:

> I think one of the best things is to actually learn from your peers. [The principal] did recognize that [and] we would spend faculty meeting days going into these four classrooms, and we're going to walk around and see what they're doing and how they're doing it and let us discuss, and I thought that was good. We were actually able to be a little more interactive with each other.

This teacher explicitly linked collaborative learning activities to the principal's decisions. She saw the principal as supporting classroom walkthroughs, which led to teacher discussions and interaction. A teacher in PPS explained that it could be valuable to learn from peers, and it also was valuable for the teacher, who was recognized for their strengths:

---

[5] We labeled some schools as *mixed*, and in other cases, we had insufficient evidence to make a determination about whether interviewees overall felt that their principals encouraged interteacher collaboration.

> A lot of times [teaching is] behind closed doors, or your best prac-
> tice isn't shared, or people don't ask for your advice, or if you give
> your advice it isn't wanted, but in this school, and this did start
> back in that time frame, we started being very transparent and
> we would have walkthroughs [with] our colleagues. Our princi-
> pal would point out, "Oh, so-and-so is doing such a great job in
> this area, when you get a chance stop by and check it out." . . . If
> somebody was struggling, whoever had a strength in the area the
> teacher was struggling in, they would be paired up to go in and
> kind of see how they could improve their practice. . . . That was
> huge on the part of the person who needed the help, but also on
> the part of the teacher who was considered that was their strength.

In comments such as these, interviewees expressed a direct connection between the described collaborative practices and their school's
leadership during the focal period—a link that was not expressed in
nonimproving schools. Moreover, they either explicitly or implic-
itly communicated that they felt that collaboration between teachers
during the focal period was beneficial to their individual learning, contributed to a sense that their expertise was valued, or otherwise supported the school more broadly.

The strength of the relationship between this factor—principals
encouraging and building structures for teacher collaboration—and
school improvement varied by site. It was most closely associated with
school improvement in SCS, where it was present in all three improving schools and not at all in nonimproving schools. The importance
of school leadership was the overarching theme to emerge from SCS
interview analysis. Teachers spoke more about their leaders in this site
than in any of the other three sites, although our interview questions
were the same, and this was particularly true in improving schools.
This factor also was closely associated with improvement in Aspire.

Principals at improving schools gave teachers a greater degree of decisionmaking power.

Interviewees at improving schools described instances in which
principals offered teachers decisionmaking authority nearly five times

more frequently than did interviewees at nonimproving schools. Within those descriptions, teachers offered substantive examples of how and why they found this leadership practice to be valuable. Interviewees at improving schools reported that their principals supported their decisionmaking in two different ways: First, the school leaders trusted teachers to make decisions about what they wanted to do with their students in their own classrooms, and second, they sought teachers' input for school-level decisions.

In terms of classroom decisions, teachers at improving schools were more likely than those at nonimproving schools to say that they were trusted to make choices about their instructional practice for their own classes. In one example, a teacher from an improving school told us that her principal encouraged the staff to try new approaches in their classrooms:

> I think we've had a chance to sort of scrap what's not working, and I love that about [our principal]. If something is not working, it's okay for us to try things. And if they work, let's keep them, and if they don't, then let's change them and always [try] to improve. I don't feel pressure to improve, like, "You need to do this or else!" I feel like I have that freedom to try things and if they work, great.[6]

In this instance, the teacher described a degree of trust the principal placed in staff members. She linked this to a lack of pressure for improvement and a sense of freedom. Teachers at other improving schools also described having autonomy in their classrooms as a form of trust offered by their administrators. For example, another teacher noted that, "When you have a principal who wants to work with teachers and also give them the freedom to do what they need to do, that obviously has a huge impact on trust and culture building."

---

[6]   When we include an excerpt that uses present tense, the interviewer confirmed with the interviewee that the subject they were discussing also applied during the focal period. For one example of how this was accomplished, see questions 5 and 6 in the interview protocols in Appendix A. Interviewers also asked follow-up questions to confirm whether interviewee responses were applicable in the focal period, and we coded for time during analysis.

In terms of school-level decisions, teacher interviewees at improving schools noted that principals sought their input. For instance, one teacher commented,

> I felt like the principal at the time knew kind of her strengths and what her strengths were not, her weaknesses. And she would ask people who were stronger in different areas, like scheduling and things like that, to help make those decisions.

In this case, the principal not only asked teachers for their input but also recognized their expertise in particular areas. An interviewee at another school said that, in an environment with many initiatives coming from the district, the principal asked teaching staff to help prioritize because it was not possible to fit everything in. She said,

> [The principal] knows that we're asked to do a lot of things, and she knows we can't do everything, so as a staff we usually choose what we think is the most important and will give our students the most bang for the buck, and that's what we focus on. . . . We'll have staff meetings and we'll talk about, "Okay, these are the things that need to be changed and we may end up having to do all of them, but we don't have to do all of them right now." . . . And we talk about it and we decide, and majority wins. Everybody may not agree we should focus on the same initiatives, but if the majority of the staff does, that's what we go with.

In this example, the principal not only sought teachers' input into decisions about what to prioritize schoolwide but also recognized the number of demands facing teachers by not requiring them to focus on all of the things "that need to be changed" simultaneously, indicating an understanding of the time constraints that teachers face. Teachers reported that principals included them in school-level decisionmaking in other ways as well. For instance, a common way that teachers were given a degree of input was through teacher hiring committees. In interviews, participants at improving schools indicated that the delegation of decisionmaking was not a burden or additional work, but instead was a positive dimension of teachers' practice.

We identified 13 schools in which multiple interviewees talked about ways that their principals distributed decisionmaking authority among teachers. Of those 13 schools, ten demonstrated improvement during the focal period. This was one of the only findings that appeared to be related to school improvement in all four sites.

As with principal-encouraged collaboration, the relationship between teacher decisionmaking power and improvement in SCS was clear, where positive associations with school leadership was a central topic of interviewee responses at improving schools. Teacher decisionmaking power was the factor that was most associated with school improvement in Aspire, where interviewees at two improving schools often and emphatically mentioned the autonomy over decisions offered to them by their school leaders during the focal period and interviewees at two nonimproving schools did not report any examples of their principals encouraging or facilitating teacher decisionmaking.

Staff Cohesion

Interviewee perceptions of cohesiveness among staff appeared to be related to school improvement status in two ways. First, interviewees at improving schools more often reported broad support for a common mission than interviewees in nonimproving schools. Second, in nonimproving schools, it was more common for interviewees to discuss divisiveness between groups of staff members than it was in improving schools. Both of these factors were linked to the cohesiveness of school staff as interpreted by interviewees.

Interviewees at improving schools were more likely to report a shared mission or common goals.

Interviewees at improving schools often commented on a common mission or a mutual sense of purpose among staff members. There were nine schools in which we identified multiple, separate instances of interviewees discussing the shared missions at their schools, and seven of the nine were improvers. The sense of agreement around a common mission appeared to offer assurance that teachers throughout the school were consistent across various dimensions of their practice, such as instruction and discipline.

Sharing a common mission was sometimes reported as keeping students' interests—rather than teachers' interests—at the forefront. One interviewee recounted,

> I think the main strength is our culture and our ability to collaborate and agree to disagree and keep the students' best interests at the forefront when we make decisions, no matter what the decision is, to make sure we're protecting students' best interests.

Implicit in this comment is an expectation that other staff members would work to serve students' interests. Another way interviewees expressed this sentiment was to say that they knew their fellow teachers were "committed."

Conversely, there were eight schools in our study in which interviewees never referred to a shared mission, vision, or purpose among staff during the focal period, and seven of the eight were nonimprovers. A relationship between shared mission and improvement was observed to some degree in SCS and Aspire. Notably, we did not identify any schools (whether improving or nonimproving) in HCPS in which interviewees reported sharing a common purpose.

In nonimproving schools, interviewees reported divisiveness between factions of staff during the focal period.

At schools that did not demonstrate improvement, references to segmentation of the staff stood out. At these schools, interviewees were more likely than interviewees at improving schools to describe divisiveness among their staff during the focal period. The divisions that were described often were associated with group characteristics; for instance, on one campus, new teachers at the school did not associate with the more-established teachers. Or, in other cases, divisions between groups of staff members were based on teachers' grade level or subject area. For example, according to one interviewee, "There was definitely a division of the kindergarten, first-, and second-grade teachers [from upper grade teachers]."

In some cases, the factions were divided based on perceived inequity in how teachers were treated by administrators. Sometimes, rifts between staff members were attributed to interviewees feeling that some teachers had been held to different expectations than others:

> In some classrooms, students, the rigor of work, the academic challenge, the behavior expectations are much different than they are in another class. . . . [T]hey're not all held to the same sort of caliber [and] that can lead to contention between staff members and sort of resentfulness.

Frustrations such as this one, in which an interviewee perceived that she had been held to a different standard than her colleagues, often were attributed to deficiencies in leadership.

Interviewees associated staff cohesion with leadership behaviors.

Although we have presented leadership behaviors and staff cohesion as separate factors associated with improvement status, they often were interrelated. One of the previously discussed leadership behaviors cited by interviewees at improving schools was principals' fostering of collaboration among staff. Collaborative interactions might have increased staff members' sense of common purpose and cohesion as a group. In some cases, interviewees at improving schools attributed their broadly shared mission to their principals. For instance, one teacher told us, "The climate at the school was like, people really wanted to give their all for the majority of years [that the principal was at the school]. Like, they were onboard, we knew what her mission was, we knew where she was taking us." A teacher at another improving school explained,

> I attribute [our school's positive climate] to pretty much [the principal] and his staff. Having people that were onboard and were 100 percent with him, or the majority were 100 percent

with him. Having people that believe in your vision and share the same vision as you do . . . we kind of fell in line with what [the principal] was trying to do, so therefore our students did.

As evidenced by this quote, interviewees at improving schools often reported that there was a sense that everyone—both staff and students—was moving in the same direction and had the same goal in mind as a result of the principal's leadership.

Conversely, some interviewees at schools that did not demonstrate improvement thought that their principal actually was contributing to divisions among staff. In some cases, teachers reported that their principals had favorites among the staff, or that *other* teachers might think that principals had favorites. For instance, one teacher recounted, "Just from hearing others, sometimes there was favoritism, but it's hard to tell because I feel like, in my mind, I worked hard, and I earned everything that I do. . . . I don't look for favoritism or a handout." At another nonimproving school, a teacher reported, "I never felt targeted, I will say that, but I did observe [the principal] target an individual who ended up resigning. He was much closer to that age to resign anyway, but I believe, I feel like she pushed it along." It is possible that the teacher mentioned in this comment had been rated as ineffective and that was the impetus for his leaving, but even if so, it is telling that this interviewee felt the administration at her school "targeted" some teachers.

Factors Perceived to Be Beyond the Schools' Control
Interviewees in nonimproving schools were more likely to report that factors outside their control influenced their school's success. There were three factors that were perceived to be beyond schools' control that emerged as relevant at nonimproving schools: (1) interviewees reported that competing schools siphoned off strong students; (2) interviewees suggested that their students' potential for achievement was constrained by such demographic factors as socioeconomic status or ethnicity; and (3) interviewees had negative reactions to student discipline policies during the focal period. Interviewees appeared to believe that these factors had at least as much of an effect on student learning as

anything within their control as educators. Schools where one or more of these factors was mentioned were more likely to be nonimprovers.

Interviewees at nonimproving schools were more likely to report that students transferred to other schools in their area.

We asked the following particularly general question in our interviews, hoping to elicit unanticipated factors that might have either stimulated or forestalled improvement during the focal period: "Were there any major events that affected your school in the period between 20XX and 20XX?"[7] We received a variety of answers to this question, including changes in the neighborhood, school mergers, and issues at district central offices. However, one response came up more than others at nonimproving schools: that students had begun to transfer to other schools in their area during the focal period. Some interviewees told us that other schools had siphoned off their highest-achieving students in particular. Responses of this nature were offered by at least two interviewees at each of five different schools. Four of these schools were nonimprovers. The only site where we did not hear about this challenge at any school was Aspire. This might be because interviewees at Aspire—a CMO—did not view competition from other schools in the same light as interviewees from the traditional public schools in the other sites.

Sometimes, interviewees were vague about why they viewed competition from other schools as problematic. For instance, one teacher said that the population of their school had changed because of new charter schools opening in the area: "There's been a lot of charter schools that have opened up. I think number three is opening up, like in the past several years. I know the population kind of changes based on that, which might change the data." Other interviewees posited that their academically high-performing students moved to other schools: "A lot of our higher-performing students left this school, they got pulled and went to other schools that were performing better, it was

---

[7]   Dates were filled in with sites' focal periods.

kind of this cycle of we're not performing well so students that were performing well left, and new kids came in."

School enrollment data did not reveal a significant decline in enrollment during the focal period at any of these schools, but that could be because students who were leaving were replaced with new students, as implied by the latter quote. Whether it was truly the case that students were drawn away from these schools during the focal period, the belief is relevant: Interviewees in several schools offered this as an explanation for what they perceived to be declining or stagnant performance.

Interviewees at nonimproving schools linked student demographic characteristics to school success.

Schools where teachers described students as unlikely to demonstrate high achievement because of their background or characteristics of their communities were less likely to be improvers than schools in which teachers did not make such comments. Interviewees exhibited these attitudes toward students when they indicated that a student's or a student's family's ethnicity, home language, socioeconomic status, or other demographic characteristics were linked to their ability to demonstrate success in school. There were 12 schools in which teachers made such comments, ten of which were nonimprovers. We did not ask directly about student demographic factors; if we had, we might have obtained socially desirable answers (i.e., interviewees might not have expressed their true beliefs, potentially out of concern about violating societal or professional norms). Their attitudes about the constraints associated with student demographic characteristics emerged, instead, from their replies to other questions.

In some cases, comments linking student achievement to demographic characteristics arose in relation to changes that interviewees perceived in their schools' neighborhoods during the focal period. Some linked a perceived increase in the percentage of low-income students attending the school to a decline in achievement. For instance, one teacher said, "We're increasing in our free and reduced [-price] lunch status, so some of our kids that used to be high achieving, we don't have that group or that clientele as much anymore." In a more-extended example, an interviewee from a nonimproving school directly linked affordable housing to challenging student attitudes and behaviors:

> This school was built about ten years ago; the first three to four years were really, really strong. You can see it in our academics. You saw that kids were coming in prepared to learn. . . . [Our area] has kind of turned into a refuge for our downtown [city] families, who can find affordable housing and get out of a situation that they feel is not healthy down there. So coming over here you just change the location, you don't necessarily change your attitude or your behavior.

This interviewee's perception was that the "downtown families" who moved into the school's vicinity were not prepared to learn, and that students coming from homes with financial hardships had an "attitude" or "behavior" that made them less ready to learn. In another instance, an interviewee at one nonimproving school told us that "It is more of where these children come from. It's hard to educate them because of their backgrounds."

Some comments mentioned students' or schools' racial or ethnic characteristics. For instance, when one interviewee mentioned declining behavior at their school and was asked when the decline began, they responded,

> I guess we got a little bit more diverse. And with that, I guess some of the kids are disrespectful and that's pretty much it. We got more diverse and with that I saw the disrespect starting to happen and it's gotten a little bit worse over the years, so yeah.

This teacher linked diversity to an increase in misbehavior at their school. In a contrasting example, an interviewee explained that the neighborhood surrounding their school had become increasingly wealthy and white and said, "We've always had good students, but the quality of the students' academic level, parental support, all that stuff has grown exactly with the neighborhood, easily." This interviewee reported an increase in the affluence of students attending the school and linked that change to students' academic ability and high levels of parental support. Despite this interviewee's perception of improvement, this school was a nonimprover according to our selection criteria.

We reviewed student demographic data on the 22 case-study schools and found that there were shifts in student demographics at some schools during the focal period, but the population of low-income and/or minority students did not increase at a rate that was significantly higher at the nonimproving schools than the improving schools. By design, our research team had restricted the pool of schools from which we drew our case-study schools to those without extreme demographic shifts during the focal period.[8] Therefore, these kinds of comments might not be reflective of actual demographic change; rather, they might reflect interviewees' perceptions that there were changes. We cannot make claims about causality, however, because it is not possible to determine (based on our data) whether biased teacher beliefs about the role of student background factors contributed to a lack of improvement or whether a lack of improvement reinforced existing beliefs held by school staff.

As with other findings, the strength of this finding varied by site. There were two sites in which this negative factor was present in every nonimproving school and was not identified in any improving schools: HCPS and SCS.

An analysis of demographic changes in HCPS schools indicated that there was an 11-percentage-point increase in LIM students at the schools that did not improve over the focal period. There was also a slight increase in the percentage of LIM students at improving schools, although this increase was only 3 percentage points.[9] It is possible that these demographic changes might have had a direct influence on school improvement, but the perceived relationship between demographics and school improvement might also—or instead—have been mediated by educators' beliefs and attitudes about students' potential for achievement. This explanation is supported by an examination of the subset of improving and nonimproving HCPS schools with similar

---

[8] For more details, see the section on school selection in Appendix A.

[9] See Appendix A for more details regarding site selection.

changes in demographics—all in the 4 to 7 percentage-point range. This subset shows the same pattern of comments as the full HCPS sample, providing evidence that it might be the *perception* of student demographics rather than the actual demographics that is associated with school nonimprovement. Although our data did not allow us to probe more deeply into this issue, we believe that this is a critical topic for further study.

In SCS, too, some interviewees at each nonimproving school—and none in the improving schools—linked school achievement to the demographic characteristics of their students and community. Unlike in HCPS, however, there were no differences in actual demographic changes between improving and nonimproving schools in SCS. To illustrate this point, at nonimproving schools where interviewees attributed a lack of success at their school to an increase in students from low-income backgrounds, the change in the percentage of LIM students attending their school was similar to the change in the improving schools. This suggests that the difference in improving and nonimproving schools on this dimension might have been more closely related to the beliefs of interviewees rather than reality. Alternatively, it might be that the school-selection measures we employed were too blunt (e.g., percentage of LIM students) to pick up more-nuanced demographic shifts.

We categorized two schools in Aspire as having interviewees that held these views, which is fewer than in other sites; one of these schools was an improver and one was a nonimprover. We recognize that the absence of comments about students' potential for success being linked to their demographic characteristics does not necessarily indicate that interviewees did not hold such beliefs; it could mean that their beliefs did not emerge in interviews for a variety of reasons. For instance, staff at some schools might have received training related to equity or cultural sensitivity and might have recognized that comments such as these could be interpreted as biased. Or, the topic simply might not have surfaced for all interviewees. As noted earlier, we did not ask about this topic directly. The connection between teacher and school staff biases and school improvement is one that we believe should be further explored. As we know from prior research, educators' expectations can affect student learning (Dobbie and Fryer, 2013; Kraft et al., 2016).

Interviewees at nonimproving schools were more likely to express frustration with site discipline policies.

Interviewees at nonimproving schools also were more likely to report that site discipline policies during the focal period were problematic, and interviewees in several instances stated that they or their administrators had their "hands tied" because of broader policies at the site (i.e., district or CMO) level. Frustration with such policies was reported at seven schools that were classified as nonimprovers and at only one school that was classified as an improver.

Frustration with discipline policies stemmed from a variety of sources. In some cases, teachers observed a lack of action taken to curb misbehaviors. In other cases, interviewees reported that difficulty with behavior was something that they or their school had attempted to address with their own approach to discipline, but it was too complex or large of a problem to be fixed. We know that there were changes to student behavior policies in at least one of the sites during the focal period where the central office pushed schools to adopt policies that would cultivate a positive culture and climate and reduce punitive disciplinary actions. Such policies were part of a larger, national trend (sparked at least in part by federal guidance during this period) toward the implementation of discipline policies that are designed to reduce racial disparities in disciplinary approaches and to be more restorative than punitive.

Some interviewees at nonimproving schools were frustrated with how behavior-management and discipline policies were implemented at their schools. Staff follow-through was one prominent point of frustration. For example, an Aspire teacher commented,

> Saturday schools weren't always happening, so there's no, like, consequence, like if you do XYZ, then it becomes a Saturday school, and then Saturday schools weren't happening, so kids

were kind of like, "This is a bunch of BS," like, "I'm not going to get a Saturday school, so I'll just act up."[10]

The ways in which interviewees described dissatisfaction with discipline policies often were framed as outside their control because student behavior was seen as a problem stemming from students' homes and not from their teachers or schools. The teachers we interviewed described situations in which they felt that they had little influence. Some interviewees thought that the policies themselves were ineffective or that implementation was inconsistent. The relationship between this discipline-related factor and improvement status was most salient in HCPS and Aspire.

Perceptions of the Intensive Partnership Levers

Implementation of IP levers did not appear to be associated with school improvement status.

The IP theory of action posited that a set of human capital strategies linked to valid teacher-evaluation measures would improve TE, promote more-equitable distribution of effective teachers, and lead to improved outcomes for students.[11] The levers of improvement were teacher-evaluation processes, staffing policies, PD practices, career ladders for teachers, and compensation policies. Our interviews explored interviewees' perspectives about the levers of the IP initiative. We were not trying to gauge fidelity of implementation; rather, we were exploring interviewees' recollections of how the levers worked, what effects they thought the levers had on their own practice, and how they and fellow staff felt about the levers at the time they were implemented. We did not find that aspects or perceptions of the levers were associated with school improvement status. Nevertheless, because they were core

---

[10] *Saturday school* refers to a disciplinary consequence for misbehavior in which students attend school on the weekend.

[11] For more information on the levers of the IP initiative, see Stecher et al., 2018.

elements of the initiative, we briefly describe interviewee responses to each of the levers.

Teacher-Evaluation Processes

As implemented in the IP sites, teacher evaluation consisted of classroom observations and measures of student achievement growth. Some sites' systems also included such elements as student surveys, family surveys, and teacher professionalism indicators. However, when we asked teachers at our 22 schools about their evaluations, they generally equated them with teacher observations and less frequently to student surveys and value-added modeling (VAM) ratings.

There was little variation between teacher opinions about the evaluation system in improving and nonimproving schools. Although many teachers we interviewed reported that feedback from observations helped them improve their performance, teachers also related many concerns about the evaluation system that closely echoed the teacher concerns reported in the main IP study (Stecher et al., 2018). At most of the 22 sites, teachers were concerned about the lack of consistency of observation ratings across observers. Teachers in improving and nonimproving schools also noted the challenge of basing observation scores on a very limited number of observations, which in turn could lead to the observation becoming what was often referred to as "a dog and pony show." In discussing other measures, teachers commented on the unfairness of the use of a school-level VAM score for teachers of nontested students, noted problems with student bias in student survey responses, and mentioned the inappropriateness of the student surveys for very young students.

Staffing Policies

We examined whether any specific aspect of staffing was related to improver status. There was not much evidence to draw on because interviewees other than principals tended not to have information about staffing policies. No discernable patterns related to improver status emerged from the data we did gather. Teachers and administrators at most of the improving schools said that teacher input was sought regarding staffing and hiring decisions; however, this also was reported at some nonimproving schools. Some administrators at both improving and nonimproving schools shared that evaluation results were used to place their most-effective teachers with the students who struggled the most. Again, interviewee perspectives on staffing policies were not unlike those discussed in the final IP report (Stecher et al., 2018).

Professional Development Practices

We examined whether any specific aspect of PD was correlated with improvement status but did not find evidence of any patterns. We identified 27 different aspects of PD that were discussed across schools and grouped them into three general categories—positive comments about PD; negative comments about PD; and descriptions of PD content, type, or frequency. Evidence across the data was sparse. For example, in some schools, there were no comments about specific dimensions of PD. The wide variety of topics and scarcity of evidence made it difficult to discern patterns.

Career Ladders for Teachers

Career ladders were intended to offer teachers paid professional opportunities to provide mentoring, support, and leadership for other teachers. Career-ladder positions were created with three possible goals in mind: to help other teachers improve their performance, to help retain highly effective teachers, and to motivate teachers to improve their own performance so as to obtain career-ladder positions. None of the sites implemented an actual ladder of career opportunities related to increasing levels of TE. Instead, most offered a limited number of discrete positions, such as mentor teacher or teacher coach (Stecher et al., 2018). We were not able to identify any relationship between interviewee perceptions of career-ladder implementation and school improvement. School staff at an almost equal number of improving and nonimproving schools reported the availability of career-ladder positions, but the positions rarely were mentioned by respondents overall, and participant perspectives on them did not vary systematically.

Aspire, however, was an exception. Teachers in Aspire were more likely to say that they did have career-ladder opportunities, although there was no aspect of career ladders that we found to be associated with improver status in this site. As detailed in the final IP report (Stecher et al., 2018), Aspire launched an extensive array of career-ladder opportunities during the focal period, and most of the comments we received in the spring 2018 interviews about career ladders were from Aspire schools. Of these, about an equal number were from improving and nonimproving schools.

Compensation Policies

Interviewee comments about compensation did not differ based on improver or nonimprover status. Across schools in all four sites, teachers expressed concern about evaluation scores being tied to compensation, particularly because they thought evaluation scores were subjective. The general attitude was that additional compensation for being a highly effective or effective teacher provided a bonus that made teachers feel appreciated and recognized but that it was not a major factor in teachers' motivation; helping students was the main motivator for teachers. Teachers who reported not receiving compensation because they did not receive a highly effective or effective rating often reported feeling "not good enough" or undervalued. Again, these findings echo those discussed in the final IP report (Stecher et al., 2018).

Perceptions of the Intensive Partnership Initiative as a Whole

Neither communication about the initiative nor teachers' buy-in were correlated with school improvement status.

Like perceptions of the individual levers, perceptions of how the initiative was communicated and the extent to which teachers endorsed the initiative were not related to improvement status. These were two factors that we had originally hypothesized would matter.

Messaging of the Initiative

It was our hypothesis (when we were still blind to schools' improvement status) that where interviewees felt the IP initiative was presented in a constructive manner—in other words, in a way that encouraged teacher growth and improvement in practice—schools would be more likely to have improved. However, early in the analysis process, we discovered that variation in perceptions of messaging appeared within schools, as well as between schools, and did not appear to be related to improver status. In other words, teachers in the same school often had very different perspectives about how the initiative was messaged. In the majority of schools, we found mixed opinions about how the initiative was communicated or we lacked sufficient information to classify perceptions of the communication.

Staff Buy-In to the Initiative

Our team also hypothesized that staff buy-in to the initiative and its levers would be associated with school improvement. However, we found that the bulk of the interviewees in 14 of the 22 schools were not supportive of the initiative, and it turned out that these schools were nearly evenly split between improvers and nonimprovers. Differences in buy-in were greater between sites than between schools within a site. For example, based on interviewee recollections about the focal period, we did not find any schools in HCPS where buy-in had been strong. In PPS, we categorized only one school as "bought into" the initiative. Conversely, only one school in Aspire was categorized as *not* bought into the initiative. In other words, based on our qualitative analysis of the 22 schools, buy-in to the IP initiative had no explanatory power in terms of individual school improvement. These cross-site differences in teacher reactions to the initiative echo findings presented in the final report (Stecher et al., 2018).

Chapter Summary

Across the 22 case-study schools within the four sites, several factors emerged as related to school improvement status. These factors included interviewees' perceptions that, during the focal period, their leaders had facilitated staff collaboration and learning, which often highlighted teachers as experts of their craft. Interviewees at improving schools also were more likely to report that their principals had asked for their input into school decisions and had given them a degree of autonomy over their classroom decisions. Furthermore, we found that interviewees at improving schools reported that their staff was more cohesive than did interviewees at nonimproving schools; meanwhile, interviewees at nonimproving schools tended to report divisions among staff. Finally, there was a set of factors outside the schools' control that interviewees at nonimproving schools said they experienced during the focal period: specifically, competing schools siphoning off strong students; students' potential for achievement being constrained by demographic factors, such as socioeconomic status or ethnicity; and student discipline policies that teachers felt were poorly designed or implemented and that hindered them.

When we look at these factors collectively, it appears that interviewees at improving schools were more likely to report that they felt that they had control over their classroom and school experiences than those at nonimproving schools—whether that was because they felt that they were treated as an expert in their practice or because they were able to make their own school and classroom decisions. At nonimproving schools, interviewees were more likely to report ways in which their students' or schools' achievement was outside their control and constrained in particular by the three external factors we noted.

These factors appeared more salient in some sites than in others. Facets of school leadership stood out as associated with improvement in SCS and in Aspire. Beliefs about students' capacity to learn or be successful, as linked with demographic characteristics, were closely associated with school nonimprovement in HCPS and SCS. We did not see particularly strong relationships between any of these factors and school improvement in PPS, although PPS contributed to the overall patterns among the 22 schools.[12] These findings highlight the importance of school and district context in understanding such relationships as those explored in our study.

---

[12] There are a few possible reasons for the lack of factors that correlate with school improvement in PPS. First, PPS included the fewest number of schools—four—while the other sites each had six, and it was simply more difficult to identify clear patterns among a smaller group of schools. Second, schools in the PPS sample were less likely to be at either the high end or low end of performance growth measures but coalesced closer to the middle range of improvement (see Table A.3 in Appendix A for more information). Differences between schools in the dimensions we analyzed, therefore, might have been less stark and more challenging to identify using interview data.

Finally, several factors that we thought would be relevant to the improvement status of our participating schools were not, in fact, associated with improvement. For instance, we probed on participants' understanding of and perspectives about the IP initiative levers—teacher-evaluation processes, staffing policies, PD practices, creation of career ladders for teachers, and compensation policies—without finding any links between their responses and school improvement. We also hypothesized that teachers' perceptions about how the initiative was messaged to them and their buy-in to the initiative would be related to schools' improvement status. As it turned out, however, neither of these factors demonstrated any relationship with improvement.

CHAPTER THREE

Survey Study

To complement the qualitative work described in the previous chapter, we also made use of teacher survey data that were collected as part of the primary RAND-AIR evaluation of the IP initiative. In particular, we used these data to look for relationships between staff beliefs and school-level improvement over the course of the IP initiative. Because we had surveyed teachers in every school in each of the IP sites in multiple years, we had a comprehensive set of data that we thought might yield a different type of insight than that from the qualitative study, which, by its nature, was limited to a small number of schools in each site. Another difference between the survey data collection and the qualitative data collection is that the surveys were conducted contemporaneously with the initiative, starting in spring 2011. Thus, unlike the interview data from the qualitative study, the surveys do not rely on retrospective memories. In this chapter, we describe the methods and results of this more-quantitative approach.

Method

In this section, we describe the method we used to look for associations between staff beliefs and school improvement. We begin by describing the scales derived from teacher survey data that formed our measures of staff beliefs and constituted our predictor variables, including a brief summary of how these measures were developed. (More detail on the development of the survey measures is included in Appendix B.) We then briefly describe our school improvement outcome variable and our estimation strategy.

Teacher Beliefs and Attitudes, as Gauged by the RAND-AIR Surveys

Findings from the surveys conducted as part of the RAND-AIR evaluation were presented in the final report (Stecher et al., 2018). Nearly all of those findings were based on individual survey items and were descriptive in nature. However, we also developed 12 multi-item scales from the teacher surveys in the interest of creating a parsimonious set of variables that could be used in more-inferential types of analysis. Built using both theory and empirical testing, the 12 scales align with the main topics and constructs the survey was focused on: specifically, teachers' attitudes and beliefs about the levers of the IP initiative (e.g., evaluation systems, PD, compensation)[1] and the district and school contexts (e.g., supportive climate and collaboration) that we had hypothesized might be related to successful implementation of the initiative.

In Table 3.1, we show the names of the scales and the items that made up each scale. Five of the 12 scales are related to teacher evaluation, two are related to PD, one is related to compensation, and the other four are about district and school context. A description of the scale development process, along with the Cronbach's alpha and other descriptive statistics for each scale, are presented in Appendix B. A more-general description of our survey methodology, including response rates, can be found in Appendix A of the final IP report (Stecher et al., 2018).

Unlike the interview protocols used in the qualitative analysis discussed in Chapter Two, neither the scales nor the surveys themselves were designed to study school-level variation in outcomes. Rather, they were designed to gauge teachers' attitudes and beliefs about the IP initiative and its components. Accordingly, although the survey analyses

---

[1]   Some of the IP levers are not represented by scales. The recruitment and hiring lever was not a focus of the teacher survey. The survey did include items about placement, tenure, dismissal, and career ladders, but these levers affected relatively few teachers, so the survey data on them are limited and thus not well suited to scale creation.

Table 3.1
Items Constituting Each Scale Formed from the IP Teacher Survey Data

Scale	Items
Supportive district climate [district and school context]	• Teachers have a significant amount of influence on decisionmaking in my district [or CMO]. • There is an atmosphere of trust and mutual respect in my district [or CMO]. • Central office administrators in my district [or CMO] are highly supportive of teachers. • Central office administrators in my district [or CMO] are highly focused on student learning. • Central office administrators in my district [or CMO] trust teachers to make decisions about their own instruction.
Supportive and respectful school environment [district and school context]	• School and local administrators have encouraged and supported my participation in PD. • I have had sufficient flexibility in my schedule to pursue PD opportunities of interest to me. • Sufficient resources (for example, substitute coverage, funding to cover expenses, stipends) have been available to allow me to participate in the PD I need to teach effectively. • There is someone at my school I can turn to if I need help improving my teaching. • My school's principal is strongly committed to shared decisionmaking. • I view my school's principal as an instructional leader.
Impetus for and impact of PD [PD]	• Influence on PD participation: needs identified as part of a formal evaluation of your teaching • Influence on PD participation: needs identified from informal feedback you have received on your teaching • Influence on PD participation: needs and interests you identified yourself • PD enhanced: your familiarity with effective instructional strategies in subject area(s) that you teach • PD enhanced: your content knowledge in subject area(s) that you teach • PD enhanced: your understanding of difficulties students commonly face or misconceptions they commonly have in subject area(s) that you teach • PD enhanced: how to differentiate instruction for students in classes with a wide range of ability levels or needs • PD enhanced: how to analyze data on student performance

Table 3.1—Continued

Scale	Items
Alignment and relevance of PD [PD]	• [My PD experiences this year] have been coherently related to each other. • [My PD experiences this year] have been designed to address needs revealed by analysis of student data. • [My PD experiences this year] have been relevant to the needs of my students. • [My PD experiences this year] have been useful for improving my instruction. • [My PD experiences this year] have provided ongoing opportunities for collaboration with other teachers. • [My PD experiences this year] have enhanced my ability to improve student learning.
Rapport among teachers [district and school context]	• The teachers at my school collaborate well with one another. • Teachers at my school support each other in their efforts to improve teaching. • The teachers at my school have high expectations for all students.
Expectations for students [district and school context]	• Most of my students are capable of doing challenging work at or above grade level. • Teachers can make up for most of the deficits and limitations students bring with them when they enter school. • If I really try hard, I can get through to even the most difficult or unmotivated students. • Most of my students have the ability to go to college eventually and succeed there.
Support for the evaluation system [teacher evaluation]	• The teacher evaluation system does a good job distinguishing effective from ineffective teachers. • As a result of the evaluation system, I have become more reflective about my teaching. • The evaluation system is fair to all teachers, regardless of their personal characteristics or those of the students they teach. • I have a clear idea of what the evaluation system views as "good instruction." • The evaluation system has helped me to pinpoint specific things I can do to improve my instruction. • The way my teaching is being evaluated accurately reflects the quality of my teaching. • The consequences tied to teachers' evaluation results are reasonable, fair, and appropriate. • In the long run, students will benefit from the teacher evaluation system.

Table 3.1—Continued

Scale	Items
Quality of the observation process [teacher evaluation]	• I have a clear sense of what kinds of things the observers are looking for when they observe my teaching. • The people who observe my teaching are well qualified to evaluate it. • After my teaching is observed, I receive useful and action-able feedback. • I have a clear understanding of the rubric that observers are using to evaluate my teaching. • The observation rubric is well suited for measuring many different forms or styles of good teaching. • There are enough observations to provide an accurate view of my teaching. • The observations are long enough to provide an accurate view of my teaching. • I have made changes in the way I teach as a result of feedback I have received from observers.
Validity of the student achievement component of the evaluation system [teacher evaluation]	• Scores on the student tests used in my evaluation are a good measure of how well students have learned what I've taught during the year. • The student tests used in my evaluation are well aligned with my curriculum. • The student tests used in my evaluation have room at the top for even the district's [or CMO's] highest-achieving students to grow. • I receive useful and actionable data from the student tests used in my evaluation. • I have made changes in what (or how) I teach based on data from the student tests used in my evaluation.
Validity of the student input component of the evaluation system [teacher evaluation]	• Students are good judges of how effective a teacher's instruction is. • I trust my students to provide honest, accurate feedback about my teaching. • I would consider making changes to my teaching based on feedback from my students. • The student feedback results help me understand my strengths and weaknesses as a teacher.
Opinions about the evaluation system (negative)[a] [teacher evaluation]	• I have experienced considerable stress this year as a result of the evaluation system. • The evaluation system ignores important aspects of my performance as a teacher. • The evaluation system is pushing me to teach in ways I don't think are good for my students. • If I received a very low evaluation rating, I would seriously consider leaving teaching. • The evaluation system makes teachers competitive with one another in ways that hinder effective collaboration. • Even if there are many highly effective teachers in a school, there is pressure to only rate a small number of them as very highly effective.

Table 3.1—Continued

Scale	Items
Fairness of compensation [compensation]	• The amount of compensation I receive as a teacher allows me to live reasonably well. • My district's [or CMO's] teacher compensation system (salary structure, opportunities for bonuses, etc.) is reasonable, fair, and appropriate. • My district's [or CMO's] compensation system motivates me to improve my teaching. • The way compensation decisions are made in my district [or CMO] is fair to most teachers.

NOTE: Except on the "impetus for and impact of PD" scale, the response metric for each item was an agreement scale consisting of four points: "disagree strongly," "disagree somewhat," "agree somewhat," and "agree strongly." The "impetus for and impact of PD" scale also had a four-point response metric, but the points were based on extent: "not at all," "small extent," "moderate extent," and "large extent."

[a] Because the items on this scale are negatively worded, a high value on the scale indicates a negative view of the evaluation system.

discussed in this chapter include many more schools than the qualitative analysis reported in the previous chapter, the survey study was bound by the content of the surveys themselves. Whereas the qualitative study set out to explore, almost agnostically, what types of factors might be related to school improvement, the survey analysis was limited in the types of factors it could explore. We viewed all 12 scales as plausible correlates of improvement and tested each on its own. That is, we did not begin the analysis with hypotheses that some of the scales might have stronger relationships with school improvement than others.[2]

Although the teacher survey was conducted in the spring of every year from 2011 through 2018 except 2012, our analysis used survey data from only 2013, 2014, 2015, and 2016 because we wanted our survey-based predictors to correspond to the mature-implementation

---

[2]   One might hypothesize, for example, that the school-oriented scales—in particular, "supportive and respectful school environment" and "rapport among teachers"—would be more likely to show a relationship with school-level outcomes than district-oriented scales, such as "supportive district climate," or those related to the evaluation system policies, which were highly specified and implemented sitewide without much discretion left to individual schools. It also was possible, however, that the site policies could have been implemented differently, or with different degrees of quality, in different schools.

period used to determine whether schools improved during the IP initiative period (see the section of Chapter Two titled "School Selection" for more details). Some scales, however, did not have values for all four years (see Table B.1 in Appendix B for more details).[3]

Because the unit of analysis in the variation study was the school, we aggregated the teacher-level survey scale data to the school level to create overall scale values for each school, combining survey responses across teachers and years. Although simply averaging each school's teacher-level scale values was an option, we were concerned that teachers' responses might systematically vary by year (for instance, as a result of the evolution of the IP initiative over time), and that if schools differed in the proportion of survey respondents across years, it could bias a school's value. Therefore, we used a multilevel modeling strategy, which we describe in Appendix B, that took into account the nesting of teachers within years within schools and the possibility of year effects. We conducted a separate multilevel regression for each scale and within each site to create the school-level values.

The school-level residuals generated by the multilevel regression for each scale constituted the survey study's key predictors of school outcome variation.[4] The metric for the scales is the original metric of the survey variables. For instance, a one-unit change in the school-based residual scale variable corresponds to a change from, say, "somewhat agree" to "strongly agree" (3 to 4 on the four-point disagree-agree response metric). Table B.2 in Appendix B presents the means and standard deviations of the school-level residuals-based scale vari-

---

[3]   In an ideal world, we would have had baseline values in addition to postimplementation values of the survey-based variables; having both would have allowed us to look at whether a change in outcomes—from before the initiative to the ending years of the initiative—was correlated with a change in the survey-based variables over the same period, but the survey did not begin until spring of the 2010–2011 school year, which for most sites was a pilot or early implementation year.

[4]   Because some schools with relatively few responding teachers have less-reliable means than schools with greater numbers of responding teachers, we computed empirical Bayes residuals, which shrink the residuals toward the mean, with more shrinkage for schools with less-reliable means.

ables for the set of schools included in our variation study analysis, and Table B.3 provides additional detail.

Outcome (Dependent) Variable

Improvement in teaching was the main goal of the IP initiative. Although there were a few different metrics by which we could gauge school improvement, we elected to use each school's average VAM score during the mature-implementation period.[5] These were standardized within each site by dividing by the standard deviation of these values and were shrunk toward the site mean to deemphasize less-precise estimates.

Only schools with any of grades 4 through 8 had value-added scores, so the analyses described in this chapter are limited to those schools, even though the surveys were conducted in a broader set of schools. Unlike the qualitative study, the survey study did not exclude schools that had extreme demographic changes. In Table 3.2, we show the number of schools included in the survey analyses.

Estimation Strategy

To analyze the relationship between the survey-based variables and the outcome variable, we used ordinary-least-squares (OLS) regression, with the outcome variable (i.e., schools' mature-implementation period VAM scores) regressed on each survey scale variable (i.e., school-level residual, as described earlier) in turn. We analyzed the scale-outcome relationship separately for each scale in its own regression and conducted separate analyses for each of the four sites in the variation study. The equation for these regressions is shown in Appendix B.

A key covariate in each regression model was the school's baseline VAM score, given that the focus was on the improvement in VAM scores from the baseline period to the mature-implementation period rather than the status during the mature-implementation period. Other covariates included school demographic characteristics (i.e., percentage

---

[5]   The method used for calculating teacher value added is described in Stecher et al., 2018. The school average is calculated by weighting each teacher's value added by the inverse of its standard error.

Table 3.2
Number of Schools That Had Both VAM Scores and Survey Scale Values and
Were Thus Included in the Survey Scale Analyses

Site	Number of Schools Included in Most of the Survey Scale Analyses	Exceptions
HCPS	183	Eleven schools were omitted in analysis of the "validity of the student input component of the evaluation system" scale,[a] so n = 172 schools for this scale.
PPS	43	None
SCS	130	Seven schools were omitted in analyses of the following three scales:[b] • validity of the student achievement component of the evaluation system • opinions about the evaluation system (negative) • fairness of compensation. Thus, n = 123 schools for these three scales.
Aspire	21	None

[a] HCPS did not have a formal student input component to the evaluation system, so relatively few HCPS teachers (and apparently none at 11 schools) indicated that student input was a component of the evaluation system.

[b] For these three scales, the first year of the scale was 2014 rather than 2013, and seven SCS schools closed or were taken over by Tennessee's Achievement School District (ASD) after the 2012–2013 school year.

ELL students, percentage of students with a disability, percentage LIM students—all measured at the mature-implementation period) and an indicator for whether the school was a middle school (typically grades 6 through 8).[6] Table B.5 in Appendix B presents the means and standard deviations of each covariate and the outcome variable.

After conducting the OLS regression for each scale in each site, we used meta-analysis to combine the estimates for each scale across

[6] We tried various specifications of the demographic covariates. We elected to use the full set (among those available and consistently defined in all sites) in the interest of having a comprehensive, common model across sites. We elected not to use school percentage race/ethnicity variables because these variables were specified differently in HCPS (specifically, the race/ethnicity categories were not mutually exclusive) than in the other sites and because the LIM variable is based partly on race/ethnicity.

the four sites.[7] This allowed us to examine three things: (1) whether the overall relationship across sites between the scale and mature-implementation VAM score was significant; (2) whether any apparent variation in the estimated relationships across sites was significant; and, relatedly, (3) whether any individual site's estimate was significantly different from the overall estimate.

Because the VAM outcome measure was standardized using school-level standard deviations, the coefficients from the regressions and the meta-analysis are expressed as standard-deviation units. Therefore, the coefficient for each survey scale variable can be interpreted as an effect size associated with a one-unit change in the survey scale.

Limitations

The method used in the survey study is entirely correlational; as with the qualitative study, the analyses do not support causal inferences. Although it helps that the survey data were collected during the mature-implementation period rather than after it (e.g., when the interviews were conducted), we still cannot conclude that a significant relationship between a particular survey scale and the outcome means that the construct measured by the scale actually caused or even contributed to the outcome. It could well be that the causality was in the reverse direction, with the outcome influencing the beliefs (especially given that the outcomes and the beliefs were measured during overlapping periods of time), or it could be that some other factor caused both the beliefs and the outcome. That said, we sometimes use the word *effect* in our presentation of the results, in keeping with standard usage, given that the scales were the predictors of interest in our regression models. In addition, as with any measure based on self report, survey responses were subject to bias.

---

[7]   We conducted the meta-analyses using the Stata add-on command *metan*. The meta-analysis is based solely on the coefficients and standard errors generated by the site-level regression analyses, not the raw data. Coefficients with smaller standard errors are given greater weight in the meta-analysis.

Results

Overall across sites, several survey scales were related to improvement in VAM scores.

The main results of the survey-based analyses are summarized in Table 3.3. Based on the meta-analysis combining the effects across all four sites, the following seven of the 12 scales were significantly ($p < 0.05$) related to schools' mature-implementation VAM scores:

- supportive district climate
- supportive and respectful school environment
- impetus for and impact of PD
- alignment and relevance of PD
- support for the evaluation system
- validity of the student achievement component of the evaluation system
- fairness of compensation.

All of these relationships were positive, meaning that higher values on the survey scale were associated with greater increases in VAM score averages. This is, presumably, what one would expect.

The largest overall estimated associations were for one of the PD scales and two of the evaluation scales.

Of the seven scales that had significant overall effects, the following three had the largest overall effects:

- alignment and relevance of PD (meta-analysis effect size 1.02; $p < 0.01$)
- support for the evaluation system (meta-analysis effect size 1.00; $p < 0.001$)
- validity of the student achievement component of the evaluation system (meta-analysis effect size 0.99; $p < 0.01$).

Table 3.3
Statistical Relationship Between Each Survey Scale and Mature-Implementation VAM Score Average, Controlling for Baseline VAM Score Average and School Characteristics

	Site				
	HCPS	PPS	SCS	Aspire	Overall, from Meta-Analysis
Survey Scale	Coefficient (SE)	Coefficient (SE)	Coefficient (SE)	Coefficient (SE)	Coefficient (SE)
Supportive district climate	0.64* (0.31)	1.41 (0.87)	1.10** (0.40)	−0.79 (0.89)	0.73* (0.31)
Supportive and respectful school environment	0.48 (0.30)	0.48 (0.45)	0.75 (0.48)	0.05 (0.27)	0.34* (0.17)
Impetus for and impact of PD	0.37 (0.38)	1.55† (0.84)	1.25* (0.57)	0.61 (0.80)	0.74** (0.28)
Alignment and relevance of PD	0.93* (0.45)	1.32 (0.92)	1.49** (0.47)	−0.29 (0.86)	1.02** (0.32)
Rapport among teachers	0.49* (0.21)	0.53 (0.34)	1.16** (0.38)	−0.40 (0.31)	0.42 (0.29)
Expectations for students	−0.03 (0.28)	−0.47 (0.46)	1.36** (0.48)	0.64* (0.28)	0.36 (0.34)
Support for the evaluation system	0.58 (0.38)	1.17† (0.59)	1.42** (0.44)	1.16 (0.80)	1.00*** (0.25)
Quality of the observation process	0.17 (0.38)	2.03* (0.75)	1.04 (0.65)	0.27 (0.46)	0.69† (0.37)
Validity of the student achievement component of the evaluation system[a]	2.84* (1.39)	0.73 (0.59)	0.43 (0.51)	1.43* (0.52)	0.99** (0.36)
Validity of the student input component of the evaluation system[b]	0.53 (0.33)	−0.27 (0.57)	1.65*** (0.42)	0.33 (0.36)	0.60† (0.35)

Table 3.3—Continued

	Site				
	HCPS	PPS	SCS	Aspire	Overall, from Meta-Analysis
Survey Scale	Coefficient (SE)	Coefficient (SE)	Coefficient (SE)	Coefficient (SE)	Coefficient (SE)
Opinions about the evaluation system (negative)[a]	0.01 (0.41)	−0.55 (0.84)	−1.22 (0.86)	1.10† (0.53)	0.00 (0.46)
Fairness of compensation[a]	0.76 (0.57)	−0.29 (0.95)	1.09*** (0.28)	0.50 (0.53)	0.86*** (0.22)
Number of schools	183	43	130	21	377

NOTES: Each table entry is the coefficient (and associated standard error) on the indicated survey scale in a regression that used school-average VAM as the dependent variable. The VAM measure was standardized within site and then shrunken using empirical Bayes shrinkage to account for variation in measure precision. A coefficient of 1 indicates that schools that responded one unit higher on the survey scale can be expected to have a one-standard-deviation-higher average VAM. SE = standard error. Shading corresponds to statistical significance for a two-tailed test: *** $p < 0.001$, ** $p < 0.01$, * $p < 0.05$, † $p < 0.10$. Each result is from a different regression model. See the "Estimation Strategy" section of this chapter for information on how each model was specified and what covariates were included. No corrections or adjustments have been made to the significance results to account for multiple comparisons.

[a] The N was smaller for this scale for SCS (123), as explained in Table 3.2. Also, as explained in the notes for Table 3.1, the items on this scale were negatively worded. Therefore, positive coefficients for this scale (such as in Aspire) indicate that schools where teachers had more-negative sentiments about the evaluation system, agreeing with such statements as "The evaluation system ignores important aspects of my performance as a teacher," tended to have *higher* mature-implementation VAM scores. Negative coefficients on this scale, meanwhile, are consistent with positive coefficients on the other 11 scales.

[b] The N was smaller for this scale for HCPS (172), as explained in Table 3.2.

For these three scales, a 0.1 increase in the scale variable (e.g., one-tenth of the distance from "disagree somewhat" to "agree somewhat" on such statements as "As a result of the evaluation system, I have become more reflective about my teaching") was associated with a

0.1 increase in the school average standardized mature-implementation VAM score.[8]

With one exception, all seven of the scales that registered as significant in the meta-analysis were significant in at least one of the sites. The exception was the "supportive and respectful school environment" scale, which was not large enough to register as significant in any site individually, but was significant ($p < 0.05$) overall. Because the meta-analyses were based on information from all four sites, they had greater power to detect effects, so an effect of a particular magnitude might not have registered as significant in any of the individual sites but could have registered as significant in the meta-analysis. Moreover, power to detect effects in individual sites varied for such reasons as different numbers of schools and how much the survey measures varied between schools. The number of scales that were significant ($p < 0.05$) in each site ranged from one in PPS to eight in SCS.

For the scales that had an overall significant effect, none showed significant variation across sites in the size of the effect, but there was such variation for some of the scales that did not have an overall significant effect.

In addition to indicating which scales had an overall significant effect across the four sites, the meta-analysis also reveals whether apparent variation across sites is significant. (See Figures B.1 through B.12 in Appendix B for more information.)

Of the seven scales where the overall effect was significant, none had significant differences between sites. Of the remaining five scales that did *not* have an overall significant effect ($p < 0.05$), there was significant variation across sites in the size of the effect ($p < 0.05$) for three of them:

---

[8]   We selected a one-tenth unit change on the survey scales for this interpretation because it is in the range of the variation generally observed on the survey scales. (See Table B.2 in Appendix B for more information.) The coefficients shown in Table 3.3, however, show the amount of change in school average VAM scores associated with a *one*-unit increase in the survey scale.

- rapport among teachers
- expectations for students
- validity of the student input component of the evaluation system.

Aspire was an outlier for the "rapport among teachers" scale; unlike in the other three sites, the effect of this scale in Aspire was negative. (See Figure B.5 in Appendix B.) In other words, schools where teachers agreed more strongly that there was rapport among teachers were actually *less* likely to increase in value added.

For the "expectations for students" scale, SCS was the differing site, with a larger positive effect than the other three sites and the overall effect (see Figure B.6). This is consistent with our findings in the qualitative analysis that in the schools we visited in SCS, certain types of comments about students' potential for achievement were noticeably associated with the schools' improvement statuses. SCS was also the differing site for the "validity of the student input component of the evaluation system" scale, again with a larger positive effect than the other three sites and the overall effect (see Figure B.10).

Discussion

> **The results do not necessarily mean that more-positive attitudes caused more growth in average VAM scores. It is possible that improvement in average VAM scores fostered more-positive attitudes.**

As we indicated earlier, we must be cautious not to infer that the attitudes measured by the survey scales caused the VAM outcomes. In fact, for some—if not all—of the scales, causality might have gone in the reverse direction, especially given that the period during which the teacher attitudes were measured overlapped with the period during which the outcomes were measured. One example where this seems particularly plausible is in the "validity of the student achievement component of the evaluation system" scale. In most of the sites, the achievement components of the evaluation system were based largely on value added, which was calculated similarly to our outcome variable. Teachers at schools that improved in value added relative to other schools over the focal period might well have been more inclined to think that the student achievement component was valid. The same might be true for the more-general "support for the evaluation system" scale.

We also must be cautious about assuming that the scales were conceptually distinct from one another. The scales were developed at the teacher level, where factor analyses suggested several distinct factors that we refined into the 12 scales. Once the scales were aggregated up to the school level, however, they might have become less conceptually distinct.[9] In Table 3.4, we summarize the pairwise correlations of the scale variables among the schools included in the analysis; Appendix B contains the correlation matrixes (see Tables B.6 through B.10).

Chapter Summary

The survey analysis examined relationships between each of 12 teacher survey scales and school improvement in VAM scores in 377 schools across the four sites. Looking across the sites using meta-analysis, the analysis found significant relationships between school average VAM scores and seven of the scales. For three of the scales (two relating to teacher evaluation and one to teacher PD), a 0.1 increase in the scale variable (e.g., one-tenth of the distance from "disagree somewhat" to "agree somewhat" on the individual statements that constituted the scale) was associated with about a 0.1 increase in the school average

---

[9]   For example, an individual teacher's opinion about principal leadership might be very different from that teacher's sense of self-efficacy—the former derives from the teacher's interactions with the principal and the latter from the teacher's interactions with students. However, when responses from multiple teachers are aggregated to the school level, there could be some association between teachers' collective feelings about principal leadership and their average sense of self-efficacy—that is, broad, shared feelings about the school climate for teachers might influence their collective sense of their potential impact on student learning.

Table 3.4
Number of Correlations Greater Than or Equal to 0.50 and Highest
Correlation, by Site

Site	Mean of the 66 Correlations (Absolute Values)	Number of Correlations with |r| ≥ 0.50	Highest Correlation	Pair with Highest Correlation	Reference Table
HCPS	0.29	9	0.82	"Quality of the observation process" and "support for the evaluation system"	Table B.7
PPS	0.29	10	0.77	"Support for the evaluation system" and "supportive district climate"	Table B.8
SCS	0.33	11	0.69	"Quality of the observation process" and "support for the evaluation system"	Table B.9
Aspire	0.31	16	0.84	"Alignment and relevance of PD" and "impetus for and impact of PD"	Table B.10
All sites combined	0.28	8	0.73	"Quality of the observation process" and "support for the evaluation system"	Table B.6

standardized mature-implementation VAM score, controlling for base-line VAM score. For instance, schools in which teachers expressed higher levels of support for the evaluation system experienced greater improvement in average VAM scores than schools in which teachers were less supportive of the system.

With one exception, all of the scales that registered as significant in the meta-analysis were significant in at least one of the sites. The exception was the "supportive and respectful school environment" scale, which was not significant in any site individually but was significant overall, with an effect of about one-third of a standard deviation.

Of the seven scales whose overall relationship with the school VAM outcome was significant, none had any significant variation across sites in the magnitude of the relationship. Of the remaining five scales that did *not* have an overall significant effect, three of them had significant variation across sites. One of these was the "rapport among teachers" scale, for which Aspire's effect was much lower than in the other three sites. The other two scales that had effects that significantly varied across sites were "expectations for students" and "validity of the student input component of the evaluation system"; for both of these, SCS had a more-positive effect than in the other sites.

Some caveats should be kept in mind in interpreting these results. First, neither the scales nor the surveys themselves were designed to study school-level variation in outcomes. Rather, they were designed to gauge teachers' attitudes and beliefs about the IP initiative and its components. Therefore, they by no means capture all of the possible school-level factors that could be associated with improvement. Second, the analyses were correlational, and causal inferences are not warranted. In fact, it is conceivable that for at least some of the relationships we identified, the causality might have operated in the reverse direction. Finally, some of the scales were correlated with one another and might have been tapping into the same underlying constructs. Therefore, of the 12 scales, the number of underlying factors that are associated with improvement might be smaller than suggested by the individual-scale findings we have presented.

CHAPTER FOUR

Conclusion

This chapter begins with brief summaries of the findings of the qualitative analyses (from Chapter Two) and the survey analyses (from Chapter Three), followed by a comparison of the two sets of findings, with the goal of gaining deeper insight than either study provides on its own. We conclude with some interpretations of the combined findings and some recommendations for others conducting research of this type.

Summary of the Qualitative Findings

The qualitative study drew on interviews with school staff from a sample of 11 improving schools and 11 similar but nonimproving schools in four sites. We found three broad factors that appeared to be associated with school improvement. Two were positively related to improvement: specific principal behaviors (i.e., creating structures for staff collaboration and learning and allowing teachers to make decisions in their classrooms and schools) and a sense of cohesion and unity among staff. The third factor, which was negatively correlated with improvement (i.e., more prevalent in nonimproving schools than in improving schools), was the perception that certain factors, such as student potential for achievement and student discipline policies, were outside the schools' control. Interviewees' responses concerning the IP initiative levers did not appear to be associated with improver status.

Two aspects of leadership that emerged as associated with school improvement were leaders' facilitation of collaboration and learning among staff members and interviewees' perceptions that their principals fostered opportunities for them to contribute to decisionmaking. Principals offering decisionmaking power to their staff was the only factor that was associated with improvement in all four sites individually. Both leadership factors were closely associated with improvement in two sites—SCS and Aspire.

In terms of cohesion and unity, the qualitative analysis found that teachers at improving schools were more likely to report having common goals and a shared sense of mission during the focal period. In contrast, divisions among staff members were reported in some nonimproving schools but less often in improving schools. There was evidence that staff cohesion was related to principal behaviors as well: Interviewees at improving schools were more likely to report that their principals encouraged buy-in to a common mission or vision or otherwise inspired joint work.

Another difference between improving and nonimproving schools was how frequently interviewees cited factors influencing student performance that they felt were out of their or their schools' control. Most notably, some teachers in nonimproving schools thought that students from certain demographic groups—implied or even explicitly stated to be low-income or minority groups—were less able to demonstrate high academic achievement. They also commented that changes in the school population over time had affected the school's potential for achievement. The association between this factor and school improvement was clear in HCPS and SCS. In HCPS, it is true that the populations at these schools did shift somewhat over the focal period, but this was not the case in SCS. In both districts, the shifts were nominal because our school-selection process eliminated schools that had extreme demographic changes.

In addition to the grounded theory-informed approach used to identify the preceding factors as related to improvement status, the qualitative study explored whether interviewee perceptions related to the IP initiative levers were related to improvement status. We explicitly asked about attitudes about the IP levers and how they were implemented, about messaging related to the initiative, and about staff buy-in to the initiative. These inquiries focused on five levers: the evaluation system, staffing, PD, career ladders, and compensation. There did not appear to be any systematic differences between improving and non-improving schools in attitudes about any of the levers, in perceptions of how the IP initiative had been communicated by school or district leadership, or in the extent of buy-in to the initiative among staff.

Summary of the Survey Findings

The survey analysis examined relationships between each of 12 preexisting teacher survey scales and school improvement, as measured by average VAM scores in 377 schools across the four sites. Looking across the sites, the analysis found significant relationships between improvement in school average VAM scores and seven of the scales. The largest effects were for two scales that were related to teacher evaluation ("support for the evaluation system" and "validity of the student achievement component of the evaluation system") and one scale related to teacher PD ("alignment and relevance of PD").

Like the qualitative analysis, the survey analysis found some differences among the sites. For instance, a scale gauging rapport among teachers, although not significant overall, had a significant positive relationship with average VAM scores in HCPS and SCS, and the effect was notably larger in the three districts than in Aspire. Similarly, a scale gauging teachers' expectations for students did not have a significant overall effect but it displayed significant variability among the sites, with a larger (positive) estimate in SCS than in the other sites. The same was true for a scale gauging teachers' beliefs in the validity of the student input component of the evaluation system.

Synthesizing the Two Sets of Results

Table 4.1 provides a summary of the results from both studies. Each row of the table refers to the association of a specific school factor with improvement in student outcomes. We color code the cells to indicate the prevalence and strength of relationships that we observe, although

Table 4.1
Comparison of Qualitative Study and Survey Study Findings

Factor	Qualitative Study	Survey Study
Leadership	Principals fostered collaboration and learning among staff members • This factor was associated with school improvement overall, most notably in SCS and Aspire Principals provided opportunities for staff decisionmaking • This factor was associated with school improvement overall and in all four sites	Supportive and respectful school environment • This factor had a significant overall effect; there was no significant variation in effect across sites
Staff cohesion	Adherence to a common mission • This factor was associated with school improvement overall, most notably in SCS and Aspire Divisions among staff • This factor was associated with school nonimprovement overall, but it was not notable in individual sites	Rapport among teachers • This factor had no significant overall effects; there was significant variation across sites, with the three districts having a greater and more-positive effect than in Aspire
Factors perceived to be outside the schools' control	A belief that other schools siphoned off student population • This factor was associated with school nonimprovement overall, but not in individual sites School staff expectations for students based on demographic characteristics • This factor was associated with school nonimprovement overall, notably in HCPS and SCS Frustration with discipline policies • This factor was associated with school nonimprovement overall, notably in HCPS and Aspire	No scale Expectations for students • This factor had no significant overall effect; there was significant variation across sites, with evidence of a large positive effect in SCS No scale
Supportive district climate	Interviewee perspectives were not associated with patterns in school improvement	Supportive district climate • This factor had a significant overall effect; there was no significant variation in effect across sites

Table 4.1—Continued

Factor	Qualitative Study	Survey Study
PD	Interviewee perspectives were not associated with patterns in school improvement	Impetus for and impact of PD • This factor had a significant overall effect; there was no significant variation in effect across sites Alignment and relevance of PD • This factor had a significant overall effect; there was no significant variation in effect across sites
Evaluation system	Interviewee perspectives were not associated with patterns in school improvement	Support for the evaluation system • This factor had significant overall effects for the evaluation system generally and its student achievement component; there was significant variation across sites on the student input component, where SCS was a positive outlier
Staffing policies	Interviewee perspectives were not associated with patterns in school improvement	No scale
Career ladders	Interviewee perspectives were not associated with patterns in school improvement	No scale
Compensation policies	Interviewee perspectives were not associated with patterns in school improvement	Fairness of compensation • This factor had a significant overall effect; there was no significant variation in effect across sites

Table 4.1—Continued

Factor	Qualitative Study	Survey Study
Messaging of the initiative	Interviewee perspectives were not associated with patterns in school improvement	No scale

NOTES: The Qualitative Study column indicates whether the association was evident overall and/or in specific sites. We say that a factor was associated with school improvement overall if the association was present to some degree when reviewing the interviews of all 11 improving schools and 11 nonimproving schools, without respect to site. We use the term notably to highlight specific sites in which the association was particularly strong. Cells shaded in orange indicate that there was no evidence of a relationship with improvement. Cells shaded in yellow indicate that there was evidence of a relationship with improvement in some sites. Cells shaded in green indicate that there was evidence of a relationship with improvement across sites.

this is intended as a heuristic rather than as an exact categorization. The two studies examined different aspects of these school factors using different methods and samples, so it is not surprising that the prevalence and strength of relationships often differs between the two studies for a given factor. Readers should check the appropriate sections in Chapter Two and Chapter Three for more details about the evidence regarding these relationships.

The first section of the table, labeled "Factors related to school and district context," lists findings related to themes that emerged from our qualitative study. These themes all had survey scales that roughly matched at least part of each theme. The second section of the table, labeled "Factors related to the IP initiative," lists findings related to the levers of the IP initiative. In our interviews, we specifically inquired about these levers, and many were also covered by the survey.

We found that the survey study generally corroborated associations found in the analysis of the contextual themes raised in the interviews. Both studies found that, in the presence of certain aspects of school leadership, such as principals fostering collaborative environments or offering opportunities for teachers to take part in decisionmaking, schools were more likely to have improved during the initiative. The qualitative study—and in some sites, the survey study—also found that schools were more likely to improve where a sense of cohesion among staff was reported and were less likely to improve where it was reported that factors outside the schools' control influenced their success.

On the other hand, the qualitative study did not find a relationship between interviewee perspectives regarding features of the IP initiative and school improvement, but the survey study did find that perceptions of some elements of the IP initiative were associated with improvement. Neither of the two studies' designs support causal inferences.

> **Both studies found that schools where leaders provided decisionmaking opportunities to teachers and where teachers had a sense of unity were more likely to have improved.**

Our strongest evidence, derived from both the qualitative and survey studies, is that highly regarded school leadership was associated with school improvement. Although leadership was not one of the levers of the IP initiative, teachers made repeated references to specific leadership qualities during interviews at improving schools. In every site, teachers in improving schools valued the decisionmaking opportunities offered to them by their principals, both in the classroom and in school-level decisions. We also found a positive relationship between school improvement and staff perceptions that principals had fostered collaboration among staff. These findings were corroborated by the survey study, which found a strong association between a scale that included several items pertaining to school leadership and school average VAM scores. Some of the items on the scale, such as "My school's principal is strongly committed to shared decisionmaking," closely paralleled interview comments from the qualitative study.

We also found support in both studies for a positive association between staff cohesion and school improvement. In the qualitative study, teachers in improving schools were more likely than staff in the other schools to report that they shared a common mission with their peers. Staff in the improving schools also were less likely to highlight divisions among staff members. Similarly, the survey study found an association in the three school districts (but not in Aspire) between improvement and a scale called "rapport among teachers," which included such items as "The teachers at my school collaborate well with one another" and "Teachers at my school support each other in their efforts to improve teaching."

The qualitative study found an association between school non-improvement and participants' references to perceived external constraints of three types: competition from other schools, student demographics, and discipline policies. Of these three emergent themes, only the one related to student demographics had a close conceptual parallel in the survey study; specifically, in a scale gauging teachers' expectations for students. This scale, which we found to be associated with improvement in some sites, included such items as "Most of my students are capable of doing challenging work at or above grade level" and "Most of my students have the ability to go to college eventually and succeed there."

The final school and district context theme highlights an exception to the similarity between the two studies' findings with respect to these contextual factors. The survey study found that staff in improving schools perceived the district or CMO to be supportive. In contrast, the qualitative study did not find that perceptions of central office support differed between improving and nonimproving schools.

The qualitative study did not find that participant perceptions of the IP initiative were associated with improvement, but the survey study found that they were.

As shown in the "Factors related to the IP initiative" section of Table 4.1, the biggest difference between the qualitative results and the survey results relates to the IP initiative and its elements. The qualitative study did not find that interviewee perceptions of IP initiative levers appeared to be associated with school improvement. The survey analysis, on the other hand, found that several IP-related constructs were associated with school improvement, both overall and in particular sites. Because the teacher surveys were designed to gauge attitudes and beliefs about the IP initiative, most of the survey items—and eight of the 12 survey scales—focused on the IP levers, in particular teacher evaluation (five scales), PD (two scales), and compensation (one scale).[1] This emphasis of the survey, and its administration during the height of the IP initiative, might have made it more sensitive to participant perceptions of IP-related factors than the qualitative study. This could help explain why, in the survey analysis, five of the eight lever-related scales predicted school improvement overall, and seven predicted school improvement in at least one of the four sites (see Table 3.3 in Chapter Three). As previously noted, however, it could be that school improvement influenced teachers' attitudes about the levers rather than vice versa, given that the attitude data were collected during the same period over which the schools were (or were not) improving.

> **The two studies differed in many respects—purpose, methodological approach, samples, time frames, and measures—so it is unsurprising that they did not yield identical findings.**

In comparing the results of the two studies, it is important to keep in mind the many respects in which the two studies differed. Specifically, they had

- different purposes: The qualitative study was intentionally designed to identify factors related to school-level variation in outcomes. In contrast, the survey study was based on surveys designed to gauge teachers' attitudes and beliefs about the IP initiative and its components.
- different school and teacher samples: The qualitative study based its conclusions on a small, purposeful sample of improving and nonimproving schools, and it is possible that the patterns observed

---

[1]   The teacher survey had hardly any questions related to staffing. The survey did have some questions related to career ladders, but because of the skip patterns on the survey around these questions and the fact that the implementation of career ladders varied greatly across the sites and across schools within the sites, the career ladder survey questions did not lend themselves to the formation of a scale.

in these schools might not hold in other schools.[2] Similarly, the teachers interviewed for the qualitative study—who were selected because they remained at their sites for several years following the focal period—might have been different than other teachers in the same schools. The survey study collected data from many more schools and teachers. (The trade-off, of course, was that the survey study did not collect the depth of information that the qualitative study did.)

- different time frames for data collection and reliance on memory: The qualitative data, which were collected in spring 2018, relied on respondents' recall of past years (two to five years prior to the interviews), whereas the surveys were conducted during the period we were studying and asked respondents about the then-present. Even so, the survey data were collected during—rather than prior to—the mature-implementation period, meaning that outcomes could have influenced attitudes.

- different methodological approaches: The qualitative study used an approach that was informed by grounded theory, which was designed to enable unexpected themes to emerge based on participant responses. The teacher surveys, on the other hand, employed predetermined, closed-ended questions with Likert-scale response options. Although some of the survey scales did bear resemblance to the leadership, unity, and cohesion factors that emerged from the qualitative work, they were by no means identical and might not have been good measures of the specific dimensions identified by the qualitative analysis.[3]

---

[2]   Exploratory analyses of the survey data, in which we interacted the scale variables with whether schools were in our qualitative sample, did not find strong or consistent evidence that the survey responses from the visited schools differed from the responses from other schools in terms of their relationship with school improvement. In fact, where there were differences, they often indicated that the factors identified in the survey study (especially the IP-related factors) were *more* associated with improvement in the visited schools than in other schools.

[3]   However, we did not find notably greater convergence of the two sets of results when we conducted survey analyses using specific survey items that most closely resembled the factors identified by the qualitative study instead of the multi-item scale composites.

- different approaches to confounding factors: For the qualitative study, we tried to pick nonimproving schools that resembled the improving schools in terms of percentage of LIM students, but the schools nevertheless varied, at least to some extent. The survey analysis, through the use of multiple regression, controlled for a variety of things that might influence the outcome, such as school demographics, although there is always the possibility of unmeasured influences.[4]
- different outcome measures: The qualitative and survey studies used different measures of school improvement. Specifically, the measure we used to classify schools as improvers or nonimprovers for the qualitative study constituted not only the change in the VAM score but also the change in mathematics and ELA test scores. The survey study used school average VAM scores during the mature-implementation period as an outcome measure, controlling for baseline period average VAM scores and school demographics. The survey study's measure, which only included VAM, might have more closely resembled the TE measure developed by the sites for their IP work. This could help explain why the survey study found that the IP-related factors predicted improvement, while the qualitative study did not.[5]

Given these many differences in the two studies' designs, it is not surprising that there were also some differences in their findings.

---

[4]   Exploratory analyses of the survey data did not find that omitting school demographic covariates or changing the covariate specifications made the survey findings consistently more similar to the qualitative findings.

[5]   In exploratory analyses of the survey data that used outcome variables that more closely resembled those used to select the schools for the qualitative study instead of the VAM outcome, some of the IP-related factors—specifically, the "validity of the student achievement component of the evaluation system" scale and the "fairness of compensation" scale—were no longer significantly related to improvement in the meta-analysis. However, the "support for the evaluation system" scale continued to have a significant positive relationship with improvement in both of the alternative outcome-variable specifications we tried.

Lessons Learned from Studying Possible Differences in Effects After the Fact

The defining characteristic of this study is that it was designed after the completion of a major intervention to investigate differences in outcomes among schools in several sites. Although there had been a comprehensive evaluation of the intervention, that evaluation was designed at the beginning to assess its overall impact and was not intended to explore differences among schools, either within or between sites. Although the overall impact was small to negligible, there was variation in improvement among schools. The present study was undertaken to learn what factors and conditions appeared to be related to this variation. An understanding of this variation is potentially as important to education as the findings of the original impact evaluation, and we learned things from this post hoc study that might help in designing future evaluations of large-scale interventions.

In this section, we provide some suggestions for the design of future multisite interventions and evaluations, in anticipation that school-level outcomes are likely to vary and that understanding this variation is an important component to understanding the effectiveness of the intervention. These suggestions arise from our experiences conducting this retrospective study, including our efforts to use previously collected data in new ways, collect new information about conditions in the past, and compare results from the qualitative and survey analyses. These suggestions also are informed by our findings (which are echoed elsewhere in school improvement and effective teaching research literature) regarding the importance of the relationships between school leaders and teachers and among teachers.

On surveys of teachers and school leaders, include more questions about school-level contextual factors and conditions that might be associated with school improvement.

The survey used in the present study was designed for the original IP evaluation and was intended to solicit staff perspectives on specific components of the initiative, mainly at the site (district or CMO) level. It would have been helpful to have more information about factors that influenced behavior at the school level. An in-depth examination of variation among schools in outcomes would require more items that focus on school-level implementation, leadership, climate, and context.

Conduct extensive qualitative data collection during implementation to support an examination of school-level variation in implementation and impact.

The present study used retrospective staff interviews at schools to investigate variation among schools in factors that are associated with school improvement. It would have been preferable to conduct interviews during implementation to elicit staff perspectives on contextual factors that enabled or hampered program implementation and outcome improvement. In fact, the IP evaluation included case studies of schools in each of the sites, and data from these qualitative efforts were helpful in understanding teacher and school leader reactions to the initiative. Insights from the case studies were used as part of the interpretation of evaluation results (Stecher et al., 2018). However, the number of case studies was small relative to the number of schools in each site, and therefore could not capture all possible dimensions of important school-level variation. Most importantly, there was no way to predict which schools would improve and which would not and thereby incorporate that into selection for the case studies.

If feasible, it would be wise to collect qualitative data from a larger sample of schools as part of evaluation efforts conducted during the initiative. Such additional qualitative data collection should certainly include interviews and focus groups and it also could include classroom observations and artifacts related to instruction and to principals' observations of and feedback to teachers.

Design evaluations to capture multiple levels of implementation and impact.

Variation in impact can occur in multiple levels of the site–school leader–teacher–student nested system. The original IP evaluation focused on variation across sites in implementation and impact. The present study focuses on variation across schools. Neither study was designed to understand variation among teachers in the extent to which their TE improved. Additional quantitative (i.e., PD participation records) and qualitative data would have been useful to understand variation in individual teachers' effectiveness and TE growth, along with school leadership's role in this variation.

Include not only more-successful schools but also less successful schools in comparative research and keep researchers unaware of schools' success status during the data-collection and coding phases.

One of the strengths of the present study is our ability to associate school-level factors with improvement in TE by comparing conditions at improving and nonimproving schools. The associations are not causal, of course, but they are stronger than those that can be made from looking only at success stories. Furthermore, it is important when studying contrasting groups to do everything possible to eliminate inadvertent bias caused by knowledge of the status of each group member. We were able to train all interviewers using the same guidelines and assign them to schools without revealing the improvement status of each school. They remained blind to school status while coding the interviews as well. This strengthened our claims about the association between identified factors and improvement status.

Conclusion

In this chapter, we have compared the qualitative study's findings with the findings of the survey study and identified similarities and differences. Most notably, both the qualitative and survey studies found that factors associated with leadership were associated with school improvement overall and in some sites. These findings fit comfortably within the larger research literature regarding the impact of leadership on student achievement and school improvement (Leithwood and Mascall, 2008; Marzano, Waters, and McNulty, 2001; Wahsltrom et al., 2010).

The qualitative study did not find support for the notion that staff perceptions of the levers associated with the IP initiative had an association with school improvement. However, the survey study found some evidence of a positive relationship between perceptions of the teacher-evaluation system and school improvement, along with evidence of a relationship between school improvement and perceptions of compensation policy, PD, and district support, although we are not able to determine whether there is a causal relationship in either direction between these perceptions and school improvement.

In addition to our findings regarding the factors associated with school improvement, we also share some insights about design features that could be used by future studies. When resources and other considerations make it possible, studies should anticipate the need to understand the mechanisms that lead to heterogeneous impact by designing in planned variation in the intervention and collecting outcomes at multiple levels of the site, school, teacher, and student hierarchy, including survey and qualitative information on perceptions and on implementation differences. Reforms that affect entire districts or CMOs require huge investments. It would be wise to learn as much as possible from such efforts, regardless of whether they succeed in their initial goals.

Methods for the Qualitative Study

This appendix begins with a description of the methods we used to select the schools for the qualitative analysis. We then discuss how we collected and analyzed the interview data and we include the interview protocols.

Selecting Schools for the Qualitative Analysis

In this section, we provide a detailed description of how we selected the schools for our comparative case-study analysis of factors associated with improved teaching.

We began by assembling information on the baseline character-istics and teaching improvement of all schools during the initiative in the four sites. Table A.1 lists the years we used for each of the sites to define the baseline period and the mature-implementation period. We calculated *improvement* as the change between the baseline period and the mature-implementation period. These periods differed somewhat among the sites, depending on data availability, but in each case were an average over three years.

Table A.2 shows the information we assembled for each school offering at least one grade of grades 4 through 8.

In selecting the case study schools, we dropped from consider-ation schools that had extreme shifts in student composition between the baseline and mature-implementation periods. We set an acceptable change threshold and dropped the school if the change in the standard-ized value of any of the last seven variables in Table A.2 changed by

Table A.1
Baseline and Mature-Implementation Years for Improvement Calculation

Site	Baseline Years	Mature-Implementation Years
HCPS	2007–2008, 2008–2009, 2009–2010	2013–2014, 2014–2015, 2015–2016
PPS	2007–2008, 2008–2009, 2009–2010	2013–2014, 2014–2015, 2015–2016
SCS	2008–2009, 2009–2010, 2010–2011	2012–2013, 2013–2014, 2014–2015
Aspire	2007–2008, 2008–2009, 2009–2010	2012–2013, 2013–2014, 2014–2015

NOTE: We used the earliest and most-recent three years of data available and averaged over each span.

Table A.2
Baseline Information Used to Select Case-Study Schools

Name	Description
Configuration	Elementary, middle, K–8 or other
ELA	Average scaled score on state ELA assessment (standardized within year and grade)
Math	Average scaled score on state mathematics assessment
Value added[a]	Average teacher value added for mathematics and ELA, shrunken (Stecher et al., 2018)
Hispanic	Percentage Hispanic
Black	Percentage African American
White	Percentage White
EconDis	Percentage economically disadvantaged
Gifted[b]	Percentage gifted
ELL	Percentage ELLs
LIM	Percentage LIM students

[a] To calculate school average of teacher value added, we first calculated a weighted average for each school of teacher value-added estimates from Stecher et al., 2018, where the weights are proportional to the inverse of the standard errors of the teacher value-added estimates. We then standardized the distribution of the weighted averages to have a mean of zero and a standard deviation of one for each site. Finally, we shrunk the standardized estimates by their standard errors using empirical Bayes shrinkage. This (1) reorders the school value estimates at each site to give more influence to more-precise estimates within site and (2) reduces the variance in sites with less precise estimates, which will tend to reduce their influence in the meta-analysis.

[b] Information about gifted status was available only at SCS and PPS.

more than that threshold. Because of the different numbers of schools in each site, we set different thresholds for each site. The threshold was 0.75 standard deviations for HCPS and SCS (i.e., the two largest sites), 1.00 for PPS, and 1.85 for Aspire (the smallest site). The change thresholds for each variable in each site are given in Table A.3. These thresholds were chosen to balance the desire for constant school demographic composition against the need for an adequate pool of schools. This step resulted in dropping 62 of 183 schools in HCPS, 16 of 43 schools in PPS, 22 of 97 schools in SCS, and 14 of 21 schools in Aspire.

We ranked the schools remaining in the pool (within each site) on their change in standardized mathematics score, standardized ELA score, and VAM score, with the lowest (i.e., most negative) change in each dimension in each site given the rank of one. We then calculated the sum of the squared ranks of the three dimensions to generate an overall measure of growth that favors schools with especially high growth in one dimension over schools with moderate growth in all three dimensions.[1] We then ranked the schools in each site by this overall measure of growth, giving a value of one to the school with the most growth by this measure. We worked from the top of this ranking to choose our improving schools. The first column of Table A.4 gives the improvement rank and percentile on this measure within the site of each of the improving case-study schools (after some schools were excluded by administrators, as discussed below).

For each improving school, we identified four schools in the same site that had the same grade configuration and the most-similar baseline mathematics and ELA test scores, VAM scores, and percentage LIM students. We measured similarity by standardizing each of these four measures for all schools, differencing the standardized measures from each of the improving schools' standardized measures, and finding the schools with the smallest sum of squared standardized differences.

---

[1] For example, consider a site with ten schools. A large number for the growth rank in any dimension indicates that the school has high growth in that dimension. Using a simple sum of ranks, a school with a rank of ten, four, and four on the three measures would have the same average rank of 18 as a school that scored six on all three measures. However, the first school would have a value of 132 for the sum of squared ranks and the second school would have a value of 108.

Table A.3
School Characteristics and Change Thresholds

Variable	Mean (%)	Standard Deviation (%)	Change Threshold (%)
HCPS (183 schools)			
Hispanic	32.7	17.2	12.9
Black	28.2	22.2	16.6
White	63.5	21.4	16.0
Economically disadvantaged	58.8	25.3	19.0
Gifted	N/A	N/A	N/A
ELL	13.7	12.2	9.2
LIM	45.4	25.7	19.3
PPS (43 schools)			
Hispanic	1.4	2.3	2.3
Black	52.9	25.0	25.0
White	37.2	22.6	22.6
Economically disadvantaged	72.3	15.8	15.8
Gifted	11.8	10.9	10.9
ELL	1.9	3.9	3.9
LIM	46.6	22.4	22.4
SCS (97 schools)			
Hispanic	8.2	11.7	8.7
Black	82.8	22.6	17.0
White	7.5	14.5	10.9
Economically disadvantaged	88.6	16.0	12.0
Gifted	3.0	5.5	4.1
ELL	7.1	9.9	7.4
LIM	84.2	20.0	15.0

Table A.3—Continued

Variable	Mean (%)	Standard Deviation (%)	Change Threshold (%)
Aspire (21 schools)			
Hispanic	60.4	29.1	53.8
Black	18.9	21.9	40.5
White	13.4	19.5	36.1
Economically disadvantaged	57.7	22.6	41.8
Gifted	N/A	N/A	N/A
ELL	29.8	23.7	43.9
LIM	52.3	26.0	48.2

NOTE: N/A = Not applicable.

Table A.4
Growth Measures of Paired Case-Study Schools

Site	Rank (Percentile) of Improver	Rank (Percentile) of Match	Configuration
HCPS			
Pair 1	3 (3)	62 (52)	Elementary
Pair 2	5 (5)	82 (68)	Elementary
Pair 3	7 (6)	99 (82)	Middle
PPS			
Pair 1	6 (23)	22 (82)	K–8
Pair 2	9 (34)	11 (41)	K–8
SCS			
Pair 1	1 (2)	42 (57)	Elementary
Pair 2	2 (3)	39 (53)	Elementary
Pair 3	6 (9)	52 (70)	Elementary
Aspire			
Pair 1	1 (5)	18 (86)	Other
Pair 2	4 (20)	14 (67)	K–8
Pair 3	7 (34)	12 (58)	Elementary

Starting with the most-improved school in each site, we looked for a school on its list of four similar schools whose improvement was near the middle of the site improvement distribution. We chose non-improvers from the middle (rather than the bottom) of the improvement distribution so as to compare our improvers with "business as usual" schools rather than highly dysfunctional schools. We proceeded down the list of improvers, and, within each improver, down the list of similar schools, until we had three pairs of schools for each site. As discussed earlier, we gave preference to improvers that had the highest sum-of-square rankings on value added and on test scores in both subjects. For the paired nonimproving schools, we gave preference to similar schools whose growth on all three of these elements was nearest to the middle of the site's distribution to exclude schools with extreme changes in any one of the elements.

We then presented our school lists to site central office administrators without revealing the pairing or the improvement designation. In some sites, central office administrators rejected schools for various reasons, and some of the schools themselves declined participation or were unresponsive to our outreach; we identified replacements as needed and possible.

The second column of Table A.4 gives the improvement rank and percentile of the final pairs. We were able to obtain only two pairs in PPS, and the contrast in improvement of the second pair is very low—the improving school was at the 34th percentile of improvement in the district and the nonimproving school was at the 41st percentile of improvement.

Table A.5 shows the average baseline characteristics sitewide for each site, for the selected improver schools, and for the selected non-improver schools. The final column shows the differences between improvers and nonimprovers as a fraction of the standard deviation of the school characteristic within the site. Differences that have an absolute value greater than one-quarter of a standard deviation have been noted in the table.

In HCPS, improvers had higher baseline scores but similar baseline value-added scores. Improvers had a higher percentage of Hispanic and white students and a lower percentage of black and economically

Table A.5
Baseline Comparison of Improvers and Nonimprovers

Name	Site Mean	Site Standard Deviation	Improver Mean	Nonimprover Mean	Difference in Means	Difference/Standard Deviation
HCPS						
ELA	-0.151	0.403	0.030	-0.046	0.076	0.188
Math	-0.099	0.401	0.069	-0.065	0.134	0.334[a]
Value added	0.007	0.051	-0.015	-0.012	-0.003	-0.058
Hispanic	0.327	0.171	0.259	0.215	0.044	0.257[a]
Black	0.282	0.221	0.083	0.220	-0.137	-0.620[a]
White	0.635	0.213	0.871	0.741	0.130	0.610[a]
Economically disadvantaged	0.588	0.253	0.401	0.494	-0.093	-0.368[a]
Gifted[b]	N/A	N/A	N/A	N/A	N/A	N/A
ELL	0.137	0.122	0.094	0.072	0.022	0.180
LIM	0.454	0.257	0.213	0.276	-0.063	-0.246
PPS						
ELA	-0.330	0.329	-0.704	-0.728	0.024	0.073
Math	-0.301	0.298	-0.736	-0.607	-0.129	-0.433[a]
Value added	-0.026	0.086	0.004	0.005	-0.001	-0.012
Hispanic	0.014	0.022	0.005	0.007	-0.002	-0.089

Table A.5—Continued

Name	Site Mean	Site Standard Deviation	Improver Mean	Nonimprover Mean	Difference in Means	Difference/ Standard Deviation
Black	0.529	0.247	0.790	0.750	0.040	0.162
White	0.372	0.224	0.140	0.171	-0.031	-0.139
Economically disadvantaged	0.723	0.156	0.853	0.890	-0.037	-0.238
Gifted	0.118	0.107	0.021	0.022	-0.001	-0.009
ELL	0.019	0.039	0.001	0.000	0.001	0.026
LIM	0.466	0.221	0.693	0.680	0.013	0.059
SCS						
ELA	-0.578	0.393	-0.363	-0.348	-0.015	-0.038
Math	-0.468	0.331	-0.300	-0.252	-0.048	-0.145
Value added	-0.129	0.109	-0.130	-0.082	-0.048	-0.441[a]
Hispanic	0.064	0.105	0.078	0.063	0.015	0.143
Black	0.867	0.205	0.781	0.774	0.007	0.034
White	0.057	0.128	0.123	0.147	-0.024	-0.188
Economically disadvantaged	0.909	0.143	0.820	0.808	0.012	0.084
Gifted	0.023	0.048	0.032	0.036	-0.004	-0.083
ELL	0.056	0.089	0.061	0.090	-0.029	-0.326[a]

Table A.5—Continued

Name	Site Mean	Site Standard Deviation	Improver Mean	Nonimprover Mean	Difference in Means	Difference/ Standard Deviation
LIM	0.874	0.180	0.745	0.716	0.029	0.161
Aspire						
ELA	0.025	0.300	-0.006	0.007	-0.013	-0.043
Math	0.171	0.247	0.085	0.184	-0.099	-0.400[a]
Value added	-0.041	0.159	-0.082	0.033	-0.115	-0.725[a]
Hispanic	0.604	0.284	0.618	0.746	-0.128	-0.451[a]
Black	0.189	0.214	0.162	0.189	-0.027	-0.126
White	0.134	0.191	0.165	0.028	0.137	0.719[a]
Economically disadvantaged	0.577	0.220	0.654	0.701	-0.047	-0.213
Gifted[b]	N/A	N/A	N/A	N/A	N/A	N/A
ELL	0.298	0.231	0.282	0.346	-0.064	-0.277[a]
LIM	0.523	0.254	0.590	0.669	-0.079	-0.311[a]

NOTE: ELA and mathematics scores are standardized relative to the state mean and standard deviation. N/A = not applicable.
[a] The baseline difference is greater than one-quarter of school-level sitewide standard deviation.
[b] Gifted information was not available for HCPS and Aspire.

disadvantaged students. In SCS, the two groups were similar at base-line on test scores and most demographics, although improvers had lower value-added scores and fewer ELL students. In PPS, improvers had lower baseline mathematics scores but were otherwise very similar. In Aspire, improvers had lower mathematics scores and value added, fewer Hispanic students but more white students, fewer ELL students, and fewer LIM students.

Case-Study Interview and Analysis Methods

In this section, we provide more details about the methods introduced in Chapter Two.

Data Collection

We conducted retrospective interviews with teachers and administrators at each of the case-study schools in spring 2018. Interviews focused on factors we felt might have interacted with implementation of the IP initiative or affected its outcomes but also included a variety of exploratory questions intended to solicit responses we might not have anticipated. We asked teachers to respond in reference to the *focal period*, which we defined as the time from the end of the baseline period to the end of the mature-implementation period. As described earlier, this was determined separately for each site based on data availability and corresponded more or less to the years of the IP initiative.[2] A case-study approach allowed us to investigate participant perspectives, both on dimensions of the initiative itself and factors exogenous to the initiative.

Participant Selection

We interviewed up to five teachers and one or more school leaders at each school. To select the teachers, we used staff roster records to identify teachers who had taught at the school during the focal period

---

[2]   The focal period encompassed different years across sites. In HCPS and PPS, this was the 2010–2011 school year through the 2015–2016 school year. In SCS, the focal period was the 2011–2012 school year through the 2014–2015 school year, and the focal period in Aspire was the 2010–2011 school year through the 2014–2015 school year.

and were still teaching at the school at the time of our interviews.[3] Our hope was to interview teachers who had been at the school since the beginning of the focal period, but there were not always five such teachers. In schools with fewer than five such teachers, we also considered teachers who arrived during the focal period. In some schools, there were numerous teachers from the focal period still on staff; in these cases, we sought variety in the grade levels and subjects taught.

We requested interviews with the current principal at each school, regardless of whether they were present during the focal period. In cases where the current principal arrived at the school after the close of the focal period, we contacted past principals to request an interview. If an assistant principal remained on staff since the focal period, we also interviewed them.

Protocol Design

We developed semistructured interview protocols to promote consistency in questions asked across schools while allowing for respondents to elaborate or offer unsolicited input. We selected interview topics based on the research team's prior experience studying the IP initiative, the levers articulated in the IP theory of action, factors from the literature that could potentially influence school-level policy implementation, and factors associated with school success from the broader literature on that topic. Examples of topics include type, frequency, and perceptions of PD; teacher buy-in to the IP initiative; and leader-teacher relationships.

Given that the purpose of our case studies was to gather information about the period during which the IP initiative was in place and during which the schools did or did not improve, we largely focused the protocol questions on that period. This meant that respondents had to recall conditions from years prior to the interview. Given the challenges of such retrospective interviewing, we began each interview with a set of reminders about what had been happening in the school, site, or community during the focal period. For instance, we noted such facts as the timing of a new superintendent beginning their tenure

---

[3]   In one case, we interviewed teachers who had left the school.

or a new principal beginning at the school. Our intention was to provide interviewees points of reference for the focal period as we continued the interview.

The initial interview questions focused on broad topics that might have been relevant to the initiative but that did not refer explicitly to it. Our objective was to elicit participants' perspectives on features of the school (e.g., school climate, extent of teacher collaboration) during the focal period without priming them to think specifically about the initiative. For example, one question was "Were there any major events that affected [school name] in the period between 20XX and 20XX?" As the protocol progressed, questions became more explicit, and we eventually asked direct questions about initiative levers. An example of such a question was "What opportunities were there for teacher career advancement in the period between 20XX and 20XX?" You will find the complete interview protocols later in this appendix.

Coding

We conducted coding iteratively in Dedoose using both deductive and inductive codes. We drew deductive codes from the interview protocol; these included dimensions of the school organization, the district and environment, initiative levers, and codes that were used to identify strengths and challenges noted by interviewees. Inductive codes were developed iteratively through ongoing calibration conversations among coders.

We divided transcripts among five coders so that transcripts from each school were coded by several different people. This limited the possibility that a school-level trend emerged from the transcripts because of individual coder bias. Throughout the coding process, the team met regularly to discuss emerging inductive codes and to calibrate using common transcripts—each coder coded the same transcripts individually, and we met to discuss any discrepancies. This process was designed to ensure that codes would be applied consistently across team members; if there was notable variation in the team's coding, we returned to another shared transcript to recalibrate. Team members involved with data collection and analysis remained blind to the schools' improvement status during the coding process.

Preliminary Analysis

Once initial coding was complete, but before schools' improver status was revealed to the qualitative study team, we collaboratively generated a list of factors that we hypothesized might be linked to improver status. For instance, based on our site visits and coding, we noted variation in the degree of teacher collaboration reported by interviewees, so we included teacher collaboration as a factor. The list constituted our initial hypotheses about which factors might distinguish schools that improved from those that did not. These factors were used to guide the development of an analytic matrix.

Matrix Analysis

After we generated the list of hypothesized influential factors, we created a matrix to organize the large quantity of coded data. In this matrix, each row represented a case-study school, and each column represented one of the factors that we listed as potentially relevant to site improvement status (which had not yet been revealed to team members working on the analysis). We then populated each cell with a summary of a particular factor at a specific school. To do so, we pulled and reviewed all relevant excerpts using Dedoose. In each cell, we included illustrative quotes, noted strengths or challenges within the cell, and highlighted any contradictions in the interviewees' accounts at that school. We conducted this process for each cell in the matrix, summarizing how interviewees talked about each factor at each school.

Once we had completed summaries for all the cells, we simplified further by labeling each cell with single words. To do so, we identified a threshold to use in each column. We set thresholds using three different types of criteria: numerical, prevalence, and quality (Bush-Mecenas and Marsh, 2018). Setting a numerical threshold was simple; for instance, a column regarding the number of principals at the school during the focal period was one, two, or more than two. Thresholds in prevalence and quality varied based on the dimension and required more interpretation. For instance, the *messaging of initiative* category captured interviewees' comments regarding the way the IP initiative was introduced to them and how it was framed by school and site representatives throughout the initiative. As we read the summary cells in this column, we concluded that the relevant variation in this category was whether interviewees felt that the initiative was messaged in a way that was constructive or nonconstructive. Looking across the summarized content and returning to coded transcripts when needed, we decided whether interviewees at each school recalled that the initiative was messaged constructively, nonconstructively, or somewhere in between. When there was a fairly even spread of constructive and nonconstructive reports at a school, we classified the cell contents as *mixed*. Finally, there were some cells for which we did not have enough information to determine directionality. These were labeled as *insufficient information*. We executed this summarizing process for every cell in the matrix. We then color coded cells to more easily identify patterns in the summarized data; for example, in the case of the messaging dimension, all cells that we had labeled as constructive were green, all nonconstructive cells were red, and those with mixed or insufficient information were without color (see Bush-Mecenas and Marsh, 2018). By viewing the color-coded, high-level matrix, we could identify dimensions of the matrix (columns) with clear variation between improving and nonimproving schools.

A key characteristic of this analyses is that summarized cells cannot be used alone to draw conclusions; matrix analyses also do not support simple frequency counts. Each cell suggests only directionality (e.g., interviewees reported generally positive or negative climate at the school during the focal period) and helps identify patterns to investigate further in excerpts and transcripts. For instance, in the category of messaging of the initiative, a cell coded *constructive* would indicate that generally, at this school, interviewees reported that the initiative was framed in a constructive way during the focal period. But there is much more detail to uncover within that category; there are a multitude of ways that messages could have been constructively conveyed. In addition, most cells have meaning only in conjunction with other information—that is, we cannot know that a cell is low in a category unless we have compared it with one that we consider to be high. In other words, all judgments are relative—relative to other schools within each site and across the entire sample.

We used the matrix to identify the categories on which to focus our more-detailed analyses. When we observed notable variation within a dimension, we returned to the original summarized matrix—and, in some cases, the full transcripts—to better understand that dimension at each site. We wrote memos about what appeared to be emerging from dimensions with notable variation. To minimize bias, coders remained blind to schools' improvement status during this phase of the analysis.

Identifying Factors Related to Improvement: Revealing the Improvement Status of the Schools

Once the coding and initial matrix analyses were complete, schools' identities as improvers or nonimprovers during the focal period were revealed to some members of the qualitative team; others remained blind to improver status so they could be called on to do unbiased follow-up analysis. Those who learned the schools' status added a column for improvement status to the existing summary matrix. We looked within each site in the matrix to identify similarities and differences between the schools that did and did not improve. We also sought patterns in improvers and nonimprovers across all 22 participating schools, regardless of the site to which they belonged.

For dimensions in which we saw patterns emerge, we returned to the more-detailed version of our matrix, and sometimes to the coded excerpts and transcripts, to build a more-nuanced picture of the dimension. One example was in the leadership dimension—schools in which interviewees reported favorable views of their school leaders during the focal period were more likely to be improvers. We considered this finding to be too broad to be of value and decided to probe further. We returned to the transcripts, selected the excerpts coded for leadership, and sorted what interviewees viewed as favorable or unfavorable as related to leadership into inductive categories. We inductively categorized excerpts within the leadership code, generating 21 different subtopics that interviewees discussed when referencing their school leaders in a positive light (e.g., school leader was a source of motivation, school leader was present or visible to staff in the school, school leader had academic or instructional expertise) and 15 ways that interviewees reflected on leadership unfavorably (e.g., school leader demonstrated favoritism, school leader was weak on discipline). This process allowed us to be more specific about the aspects of leadership that mattered in relationship to improver and nonimprover status. We repeated this process with the other categories that emerged as correlated with school status. Throughout this process, emerging patterns were checked not only for confirming evidence but also for disconfirming evidence— when a pattern surfaced in the data, we sought examples in which this pattern did *not* hold true.

Although our analysis required that we break complex dimensions of schools and school environments down into specific elements, it was by viewing the evidence as a cohesive body that we were able to make sense of the findings. We held regular conversations as a team to discuss our developing qualitative findings and the relationship between these findings and our broader understanding of the initiative. The findings described in this report are the result of these processes.

Case-Study Interview Protocol

Teacher Interview Protocol
We are speaking to teachers who have worked at their school for five or more years in a variety of grades and subjects (as possible)

Teacher interview questions [45 minutes]
▸ signifies priority question

Background and context [5 minutes]
These questions are intended to situate the participant within the school and its history.

1. ▸ Can you tell me about your role at [school]?
   a. *If not covered:* What grades or subjects do you teach?

2. ▸ What year did you begin working here? [NOTE DATE: 20____]
   a. Has your position changed over that time? How?

Open-ended school-level questions [10 minutes]

Try not to elicit about IP specifically, but instead understand more broadly what the participant sees as important characteristics of the school and major changes in the (relatively) recent past.

3.   ▶What do you see as the primary strengths of [school]?

4.   ▶What do you see as the biggest challenges, limitations, or weaknesses [school] is facing?
      a.   How, if at all, has the school tried to address these challenges?

Now we are going to shift gears a little bit and ask about a particular time frame in the past, the 20XX–20XX school year through the 20XX–20XX school year.[4] To help you remember, here are a few facts about what was happening during this period at your school or in your district or CMO [*insert memory-joggers prior to interview*].

5.   ▶You said the primary strengths of your school are [XYZ]. Are these strengths that have changed since [20XX], or have they remained fairly constant? *Ask for specifics and examples, including when the change[s] occurred.*

6.   ▶You said the primary challenges, limitations, or weaknesses of your school are [XYZ]. Have these changed since [20XX], or have they remained fairly constant? *Ask for specifics and examples, including when the change[s] occurred.*

7.   ▶Now thinking broadly, how has your school changed since [20XX]? *Ask for specifics and examples, including when the change[s] occurred.*
      a.   *If not addressed:* How has student achievement changed, if at all?
      b.   *If not addressed:* How has teacher effectiveness changed, if at all?

---

4   References to dates in the interview protocol were filled with the focal period at each site.

   c.   ▶To what do you attribute these changes?

8. Were there any major events that affected [school] in the period between 20XX and 20XX? *Probe: We're thinking about events that may have changed the trajectory the school was on—for instance, a major storm, a new school opening nearby, anything along those lines.*

Organizational dimensions [15 minutes]

These are slightly more-focused questions about areas that literature suggests may have influenced the implementation of IP but are not directly related to the levers of the initiative.

9.   ▶What major initiatives did your school and district undertake during the period between 20XX and 20XX? *Ask for specifics and examples.*
   a.   ▶How did these initiatives influence how you teach, if at all?
   b.   ▶How did leadership communicate about these initiatives? *Probe: Were they supportive of the initiatives, negative about them, providing lip service?*
   c.   How did staff members at [school] react to [new initiatives]?
   d.   ▶Do you think [new initiatives] were successful? Why or why not?

10. To what extent did teachers collaborate at [school] in the period between 20XX and 20XX? *Ask for specifics and examples.*
   a.   How has teacher collaboration changed since that time, if at all?

11. In the period between 20XX and 20XX, what role did teachers play in decisionmaking at [school], if any? *Ask for specifics and examples; types of decisions (e.g., hiring, PD, scheduling).*
   a.   How have teachers' roles in decisionmaking changed since that time, if at all?

12. ▶How would you describe the leadership at [school] in the period between 20XX and 20XX? *Probe: Instructional support, administrative organization, behavior management, community interaction, etc.*

    a. ▶What was the relationship like between staff and administrators, generally?

    b. ▶ How has the relationship between staff and administrators changed since that time, if at all?

13. ▶How would you describe the climate at [school] in the period between 20XX and 20XX? *If explanation is needed: By climate, we mean the ways that staff treat one another, whether they are happy to come to work, the general atmosphere, etc.*

    a. What do you think contributed to such a climate? [*regardless of positive or negative*]

    b. ▶ How has school climate changed since that time, if at all?

Domains of the initiative [15 minutes]
These questions probe around IP levers.

14. ▶What kinds of professional development did you receive in the period between 20XX and 20XX? We're thinking of PD broadly, to include coaching, professional learning communities, and other training. *Probe: How often did you receive training? Was PD generally whole-school, by department, or individual? What kinds of topics were covered?*

    a. ▶In what ways did you change your teaching in response to PD, if at all? *Ask for specifics and examples.*

    b. How has professional development at [school] changed since that time, if at all?

       ◦ Do you see these changes as improvements? Why or why not?

15. ▶In the period between 20XX and 20XX, how were you evaluated as a teacher in [school]? *Probe: What measures contributed to*

the evaluation [teacher observation, surveys, student achievement], how often did it happen, and who conducted the evaluation?
a. ▶Do you remember any major shifts in how you were evaluated during that time?
b. ▶To what extent did teachers at the time seem to buy in to the evaluation system?
  ◦ What concerns did teachers have? *or* What about the evaluation did teachers value?
c. ▶How did results from these evaluations affect you? *Probe: bonuses, salary, promotions, specific training, etc.*
d. ▶What components of the evaluation were the most useful to your teaching?
e. ▶What components of the evaluation were the least useful to your teaching?
f. To what extent did the evaluation rubric measure the "correct" dimensions for improving teacher effectiveness?
g. ▶What kind of messages did you receive from administration about these evaluations at that time? *Probe on whether they seemed supportive of the evaluation system, negative about it, or provided lip service.*
h. ▶How has the evaluation system changed since that time, if at all? *Probe: number of observations, observation rubric, measures weighted in evaluation, professional development as linked to the evaluations, etc.*
  ◦ Do you see these changes as improvements, and why or why not?

16. ▶How were decisions about teacher tenure or contract renewal made in the period between 20XX and 20XX?
a. ▶Were there opportunities for career advancement for teachers at that time? Can you give an example? *Probe: Were instructional leadership positions available?*
b. Have opportunities for teachers' career advancement changed since then?
  ◦ Do you see these changes as improvements, and why or why not?

Closing questions [5 minutes]

17. Is there anything else important about [school] that I did not ask about?

Administrator Interview Protocol
For administrators at the school during the time of the initiative and *currently there*

Administrator interview questions [60 minutes]

Background and context [5 minutes]
These questions are intended to situate the participant within the school and its history.

1. What year did you begin working at [school]? [NOTE DATE: 20____]
    a. Has your position changed over that time? How?

Open-ended school-level questions [8 minutes]
Try not *to elicit answers about IP specifically, but instead understand more broadly what the participant sees as important characteristics of the school and major changes in the (relatively) recent past.*

2. What do you see as the primary strengths of [school]?

3. What do you see as the biggest challenges, limitations, or weaknesses [school] is facing?
    a. How, if at all, has the school tried to address these challenges?

Now we are going to shift gears a little bit and ask about a particular time frame in the past, the 20XX–20XX school year through the 20XX–20XX school year. To help you remember, here are a few facts about what was happening during this period at your school or in your district or CMO [*insert memory-joggers prior to interview*].

4. You said the primary strengths of your school are [XYZ]. Are these strengths that have changed since [20XX], or have they remained fairly constant? *Ask for specifics and examples, including when the change occurred.*

5. You said the primary challenges, limitations, or weaknesses of your school are [XYZ]. Have these changed since [20XX], or have they remained fairly constant? *Ask for specifics and examples, including when the change occurred.*

6. Now thinking broadly, how has your school changed since [20XX]? *Ask for specifics and examples, including when the change[s] occurred.*
   a. *If not addressed:* How has student achievement changed, if at all?
   b. *If not addressed:* How has teacher effectiveness changed, if at all?
   c. To what do you attribute these changes?

7. Were there any major events that affected [school] in the period between 20XX and 20XX? *Probe: We're thinking about events that may have changed the trajectory the school was on—for instance, a major storm, a new school opening nearby, anything along those lines.*

Organizational dimensions [15 minutes]
   These are slightly more-focused questions about areas that literature suggests may have influenced implementation of IP but are not directly related to the levers of the initiative.

8. What major initiatives did your school and district undertake in the period between 20XX and 20XX? *Ask for specifics and examples.*
   a. How did staff members at [school] react to [new initiatives]?
   b. To what extent did you support these initiatives?
   c. Do you think [each new initiative] was successful at your school? Why or why not?

9. Thinking back, what kind of support did you receive from the district or CMO office in the period between 20XX and 20XX? *Ask for specifics and examples.*
   a. How often would you say you interacted with the district or CMO office at that time? This could be by phone, via email, or in person.
      ◦ Who were you typically speaking with?
      ◦ What were these conversations typically about?
   b. Has anything about your communication with the district or CMO changed since that time?
      ◦ Do you see these changes as improvements? Why or why not?

10. How collaborative were teachers at [school] in the period between 20XX and 20XX? *Ask for specifics and examples.*
    a. How has teacher collaboration changed since that time, if at all?

11. How would you describe the climate at [school] in the period between 20XX and 20XX? *If explanation is needed: By climate, we mean the ways that staff treat one another, whether they are happy to come to work, the general atmosphere, etc.*
    a. What do you think contributed to such a climate? [*regardless of positive or negative*]
    b. How has the school climate changed since that time, if at all?
       ◦ Do you see these changes as improvements? Why or why not?

Domains of the initiative [15 minutes]
These questions probe around IP levers.

12. What kinds of professional development did teachers receive at [school] in the period between 20XX and 20XX? We're thinking about PD broadly, to include group training but also coaching, professional learning communities, and so forth. *Probe:*

How often did they receive the various types of PD? Was PD generally whole-school, by department, or individual? What kinds of topics were covered?

   a. How has professional development at [school] changed since that time, if at all?

       ◦ Do you see these changes in professional development as improvements? Why or why not?

13. In the period between 20XX and 20XX, how were teachers evaluated at [school]?

   a. What do you think was the primary goal of the evaluation system? *Probe: improving teacher effectiveness, improving student achievement, informing staffing and placement decisions, etc.*

   b. Do you believe the teacher-evaluation system improved teacher effectiveness? Why or why not?

   c. To what extent did teachers at [school] seem to buy into the evaluation system?

       ◦ What concerns did they express? *or* What about the evaluation did teachers value?

   d. How did results from these evaluations affect teachers?

       ◦ *If not covered:* Did evaluation scores influence whether teachers received bonuses, salary increases, or promotions?

       ◦ *If not covered:* Did evaluations influence decisions about teacher tenure or contract renewal?

       ◦ *If not covered:* To what extent did teacher-evaluation results drive PD activities?

       ◦ *If not covered:* How often were teachers placed on improvement plans?

   e. How has the teacher-evaluation system changed since that time, if at all?

       ◦ Do you see these updates to the teacher-evaluation system as improvements? Why or why not?

14. In the period between 20XX and 20XX, what factors would you consider when assigning teachers to classes? *Probes: content expertise, scheduling constraints, prior experience, students' academic levels, teacher evaluation.*
    a. Did certain groups of students get paired with certain teachers? *Probe: How are teachers selected to teach remedial or gifted classes?*

15. What opportunities were there for teacher career advancement in the period between 20XX and 20XX? *Probe: Were instructional leadership positions available?*
    a. How have opportunities for teachers to advance their careers changed since that time, if at all?

Closing questions [5 minutes]

16. Is there anything else important about the period between 20XX and 20XX that I did not ask about?

17. Is there anything else important about [school] that I did not ask?

Methods for the Survey Study

Development of the Scales from the IP Teacher Surveys

In early spring 2016, we developed a set of survey scales from the IP teacher survey data collected in 2011, 2013, 2014, and 2015.[1] We began with factor analyses to identify survey items—nearly all Likert scale–type items with four response options—that hung together among sets of items seen by a common set of respondents. (Because of skip patterns and screening questions, some sections of the survey were limited to certain respondents.) We then refined the suggested factors into 12 distinct scales using our judgment and iterative alpha reliability testing. At the time, the primary purpose of the scale development was to inform the content of the 2016 spring survey. This survey was going to be shorter than the survey that had been used in 2015, and we wanted to make sure to keep items that contributed strongly to scales to allow for possible future analyses that might benefit from scales or data reduction in general.[2]

Once the 12 scales were established, our next step, which we completed after the 2016 survey data were collected, was to impute small amounts of missing data on the individual survey items that constituted each scale. We did this separately within each year (2011, 2013, 2014, 2015, and 2016) using Stata's *mi impute chained (ologit)* command so that the imputed item values would incorporate random error

---

[1] There was no teacher survey in 2012.

[2] For the main IP evaluation study, nearly all survey analyses were of individual survey items (see Stecher et al., 2018).

The imputation model for each scale included all the items constituting the scale, along with indicators for site (for all seven sites in the IP initiative), more than two years of teaching experience, teaching a core subject area, school level, and school LIM status. We imputed missing values only for teachers who answered all but one (or in some cases two) of the items constituting a particular scale.[3] We constructed the scales by simply averaging the component items using the *generate* option of Stata's *alpha* command.[4] We present basic information about the 12 scales in Table B.1.

Creation of School-Level Values for Each Scale

To derive school-level values for each scale, we regressed the teacher-level values on indicators for year (i.e., controlling for year effects) in a site-specific multilevel model that accounted for the nesting of teachers within years within schools.[5] We then generated the school-level residual from this regression to create a value for each school on each

---

[3]   We allowed imputation of one missing item per scale on the nine scales that were composed of six or fewer items; on the remaining three scales, which were each composed of eight items, we allowed imputation of one or two missing items. We did not impute responses or calculate a scale value for surveys that had more than the allowable number of missing items on the scale.

[4]   Any items that contributed negatively to a scale would have been reversed in the averaging but, as it happens, none of our 12 scales had any items that entered negatively. However, one of the scales ("opinions about the evaluation system [negative]") consisted entirely of negatively worded items. It worked better, reliability-wise, to have separate scales for positive and negative opinions about the evaluation system than to have a single scale with the negative items reversed. This is because the negatively worded items did not function as well as the positively worded items. Whereas the individual-year alphas for the "support for the evaluation system" scale, which consisted of positively worded items, were about 0.9, the alphas for the negative scale were only about 0.7.

[5]   These regressions, which used the Stata command *mixed*, included weights that accounted both for sampling and nonresponse, but the analyses did not take into account other aspects of the sampling design, such as finite population corrections. In addition, it is worth noting that each year, we sampled teachers within schools and did not attempt to follow teachers longitudinally. Although some teachers might have wound up in the survey sample in multiple years, especially in the smaller sites, this was not by design, and we considered each year's sample to be independent of other years' samples in terms of the individuals surveyed.

Table B.1
Characteristics of the Scales Formed from the IP Teacher Survey Data

Scale	Number of Items	Number of Years Included (Specific Years)	Mean (SD)	Cronbach's Alpha	N
Supportive district climate	5	4 (2013, 2014, 2015, 2016)	2.46 (0.80)	0.90	14,295
Supportive and respectful school environment	6	4 (2013, 2014, 2015, 2016)	3.01 (0.70)	0.83	14,140
Impetus for and impact of PD	8	4 (2013, 2014, 2015, 2016)	2.67 (0.67)	0.86	14,227
Alignment and relevance of PD	6	4 (2013, 2014, 2015, 2016)	2.94 (0.66)	0.89	14,256
Rapport among teachers	3	4 (2013, 2014, 2015, 2016)	3.37 (0.64)	0.84	14,383
Expectations for students	4	3 (2013, 2015, 2016)	2.74 (0.65)	0.72	10,472
Support for the evaluation system	8	4 (2013, 2014, 2015, 2016)	2.53 (0.66)	0.90	13,157
Quality of the observation process	8	4 (2013, 2014, 2015, 2016)	3.07 (0.61)	0.86	13,233
Validity of the student achievement component of the evaluation system	5	3 (2014, 2015, 2016)	2.68 (0.66)	0.81	5,930
Validity of the student input component of the evaluation system	4	4 (2013, 2014, 2015, 2016)	2.69 (0.73)	0.85	8,672
Opinions about the evaluation system (negative)	6	3 (2014, 2015, 2016)	2.68 (0.61)	0.68	9,805

Table B.1—Continued

Scale	Number of Items	Number of Years Included (Specific Years)	Mean (SD)	Cronbach's Alpha	N
Fairness of compensation	4	3 (2014, 2015, 2016)	2.26 (0.75)	0.85	10,559

NOTES: The statistics (means and standard deviations, alphas, and Ns) are based on the scales including imputed items across all years noted. They are based on teachers surveyed in all regular public schools (of all levels) in all seven IP sites, not just the four sites that are the focus of this report. For simplicity, the statistics presented in this table do not take site or sampling weights into account. SD = standard deviation.

scale across all the years shown in Table B.1, corresponding more or less to the mature-implementation period. Stata's *mixed* postestimation prediction of residuals calculates the best linear unbiased predictions of the random effects; that is, residuals are shrunken so that schools with extreme values are moved closer to the mean if they have fewer teachers or years, reflecting that we have less real information for such schools.[6]

The school-level residuals-based scale variables are, by definition, centered around the site mean, so the average value for each site is approximately zero. Table B.2 presents the means and standard deviations of the school-level residuals-based scale variables for the subset of schools included in our variation study analysis. (See Chapter Three for a discussion of which schools were included.) The standard deviation is generally around 0.1, with a few larger values, so a typical school might be one- or two-tenths above or below the district average on a scale.

Table B.3 presents the variance components, intracluster correlation coefficients (ICCs), and school-level reliabilities for the regressions that produced the school-level values for each scale.[7] The reliability can be thought of as the interrater reliability among teachers within each school. It indicates the extent to which there is a consensus among

---

[6] Such residuals also are called *empirical Bayes estimates and shrunken residuals*.

[7] These regressions included all schools in each site, not just the subset of schools included in the variation study.

Table B.2
Means and Standard Deviations for the School-Level Residuals-Based Scale Variables for the Sample of Schools Included in the Variation Study Analysis

	Site			
	HCPS	PPS	SCS	Aspire
Scale	Mean (SD)	Mean (SD)	Mean (SD)	Mean (SD)
Supportive district climate	0.006 (0.120)	0.005 (0.077)	0.012 (0.121)	−0.008 (0.055)
Supportive and respectful school environment	0.002 (0.117)	0.002 (0.155)	−0.001 (0.100)	0.001 (0.168)
Impetus for and impact of PD	0.006 (0.107)	0.019 (0.099)	0.026 (0.089)	-0.018 (0.058)
Alignment and relevance of PD	0.009 (0.081)	0.006 (0.077)	0.025 (0.101)	−0.005 (0.057)
Rapport among teachers	0.025 (0.189)	0.021 (0.194)	0.023 (0.129)	0.035 (0.193)
Expectations for students	0.026 (0.156)	0.067 (0.175)	0.008 (0.102)	0.078 (0.180)
Support for the evaluation system	0.000 (0.093)	0.007 (0.115)	0.010 (0.108)	-0.008 (0.049)
Quality of the observation process	0.005 (0.095)	0.010 (0.084)	0.010 (0.075)	0.003 (0.102)
Validity of the student achievement component of the evaluation system[a]	0.001 (0.025)	0.001 (0.119)	0.011 (0.103)	−0.006 (0.080)
Validity of the student input component of the evaluation system[b]	−0.008 (0.110)	0.001 (0.117)	−0.004 (0.115)	−0.049 (0.185)
Opinions about the evaluation system (negative)[a]	0.017 (0.087)	0.007 (0.079)	0.005 (0.058)	0.003 (0.090)
Fairness of compensation[a]	0.000 (0.061)	−0.008 (0.070)	0.003 (0.171)	−0.019 (0.085)

Table B.2—Continued

	Site			
	HCPS	PPS	SCS	Aspire
Scale	Mean (SD)	Mean (SD)	Mean (SD)	Mean (SD)
Number of schools	183	43	130	21

NOTES: The regressions that produced the residuals included every school in the site, not just the subset of schools included in the variation analysis (i.e., the schools that had VAM score values). The figures presented in this table are limited to the schools included in the variation analysis, so the means shown are not zero. SD = standard deviation.

[a] The N was smaller for this scale for SCS (123). This is because, unlike most of the other scales, the first year of this scale was 2014 rather than 2013, and seven SCS schools closed or were taken over by the ASD after the 2012–2013 school year.

[b] The N was smaller for this scale for HCPS (172). HCPS did not have a formal student input component to the evaluation system, so relatively few HCPS teachers (and apparently none at 11 schools) indicated that student input was a component of the evaluation system.

teachers in each school. It is *not* comparable to Cronbach's alpha, which measures the agreement among items within a scale. Table B.4 shows the average number of teacher respondents per school (combined across years) that were included in the regressions.

Equation for the Survey Scale Analyses

The analytic model had the following general specification:

$$Y_i^{post} = \beta_0 + \beta_1 Scale_i + \beta_2 Y_i^{pre} + \beta_3 XP_i + r_i,$$

where Y_i^{post} is the school-average mature-implementation period VAM score for school i and Y_i^{pre} is the school's baseline VAM score. $Scale_i$ is the school value (school-level residual) on the scale being analyzed, XP represents a set of school-level covariates (student body percentage ELL, percentage with a disability, and percentage LIM—all measured at the mature-implementation period, along with a dichotomous indi-

Table B.3
Variance Components, Intracluster Correlation Coefficients, and School-Level Reliabilities from the Multilevel Regressions That Produced the School-Level Scale Values

Scale	Site			
	HCPS	PPS	SCS	Aspire
Supportive district climate				
School-level variance	0.03	0.02	0.04	0.01
Year-within-school variance	0.13	0.04	0.12	0.06
Residual (teacher-level) variance	0.39	0.42	0.53	0.34
School ICC	0.06	0.04	0.05	0.03
Year-within-school ICC	0.23	0.09	0.18	0.15
Residual (teacher-level) ICC	0.71	0.88	0.77	0.82
School reliability	0.39	0.47	0.39	0.35
Supportive and respectful school environment				
School-level variance	0.03	0.04	0.03	0.04
Year-within-school variance	0.12	0.09	0.10	0.06
Residual (teacher-level) variance	0.32	0.38	0.37	0.30
School ICC	0.06	0.08	0.05	0.09
Year-within-school ICC	0.26	0.18	0.20	0.16
Residual (teacher-level) ICC	0.67	0.75	0.75	0.75
School reliability	0.38	0.55	0.37	0.58

Table B.3—Continued

Scale	Site			
	HCPS	PPS	SCS	Aspire
Impetus for and impact of PD				
School-level variance	0.03	0.02	0.02	0.01
Year-within-school variance	0.09	0.04	0.08	0.04
Residual (teacher-level) variance	0.28	0.36	0.33	0.35
School ICC	0.07	0.05	0.05	0.02
Year-within-school ICC	0.22	0.10	0.19	0.11
Residual (teacher-level) ICC	0.71	0.85	0.76	0.87
School reliability	0.41	0.52	0.38	0.28
Alignment and relevance of PD				
School-level variance	0.02	0.01	0.03	0.01
Year-within-school variance	0.09	0.05	0.08	0.05
Residual (teacher-level) variance	0.28	0.38	0.34	0.30
School ICC	0.05	0.03	0.06	0.03
Year-within-school ICC	0.23	0.11	0.18	0.13
Residual (teacher-level) ICC	0.72	0.86	0.77	0.84
School reliability	0.33	0.41	0.41	0.30
Rapport among teachers				
School-level variance	0.06	0.06	0.03	0.04

Table B.3—Continued

| | Site | | | |
Scale	HCPS	PPS	SCS	Aspire
Year-within-school variance	0.11	0.03	0.07	0.04
Residual (teacher-level) variance	0.31	0.29	0.27	0.22
School ICC	0.12	0.15	0.09	0.14
Year-within-school ICC	0.24	0.09	0.19	0.13
Residual (teacher-level) ICC	0.64	0.77	0.72	0.73
School reliability	0.55	0.78	0.52	0.70
Expectations for students				
School-level variance	0.05	0.08	0.03	0.05
Year-within-school variance	0.09	0.03	0.09	0.03
Residual (teacher-level) variance	0.30	0.33	0.32	0.27
School ICC	0.11	0.17	0.07	0.14
Year-within-school ICC	0.21	0.07	0.20	0.09
Residual (teacher-level) ICC	0.68	0.76	0.73	0.77
School reliability	0.47	0.79	0.36	0.68
Support for the evaluation system				
School-level variance	0.02	0.03	0.03	0.01
Year-within-school variance	0.11	0.04	0.08	0.04
Residual (teacher-level) variance	0.31	0.36	0.33	0.26

Table B.3—Continued

Scale	Site			
	HCPS	PPS	SCS	Aspire
School ICC	0.05	0.06	0.06	0.03
Year-within-school ICC	0.24	0.09	0.19	0.14
Residual (teacher-level) ICC	0.71	0.85	0.75	0.83
School reliability	0.32	0.55	0.40	0.29
Quality of the observation process				
School-level variance	0.02	0.02	0.02	0.02
Year-within-school variance	0.09	0.04	0.06	0.04
Residual (teacher-level) variance	0.28	0.29	0.24	0.25
School ICC	0.06	0.05	0.05	0.05
Year-within-school ICC	0.23	0.10	0.20	0.12
Residual (teacher-level) ICC	0.72	0.85	0.74	0.82
School reliability	0.36	0.48	0.37	0.47
Validity of the student achievement component of the evaluation system				
School-level variance	0.01	0.04	0.03	0.02
Year-within-school variance	0.13	0.05	0.14	0.07
Residual (teacher-level) variance	0.29	0.30	0.28	0.32
School ICC	0.01	0.09	0.07	0.04
Year-within-school ICC	0.31	0.14	0.30	0.17

Table B.3—Continued

Scale		Site		
	HCPS	PPS	SCS	Aspire
Residual (teacher-level) ICC	0.68	0.77	0.63	0.79
School reliability	0.08	0.49	0.29	0.28
Validity of the student input component of the evaluation system				
School-level variance	0.04	0.03	0.03	0.05
Year-within-school variance	0.28	0.05	0.13	0.03
Residual (teacher-level) variance	0.14	0.42	0.44	0.36
School ICC	0.09	0.05	0.06	0.10
Year-within-school ICC	0.60	0.09	0.22	0.06
Residual (teacher-level) ICC	0.30	0.85	0.72	0.84
School reliability	0.29	0.49	0.36	0.68
Opinions about the evaluation system (negative)				
School-level variance	0.02	0.02	0.01	0.02
Year-within-school variance	0.08	0.03	0.08	0.02
Residual (teacher-level) variance	0.25	0.29	0.28	0.33
School ICC	0.07	0.05	0.03	0.05
Year-within-school ICC	0.24	0.10	0.21	0.06
Residual (teacher-level) ICC	0.70	0.85	0.75	0.89
School reliability	0.33	0.42	0.21	0.43

Table B.3—Continued

Scale	Site			
	HCPS	PPS	SCS	Aspire
Fairness of compensation				
School-level variance	0.02	0.02	0.05	0.02
Year-within-school variance	0.11	0.06	0.10	0.06
Residual (teacher-level) variance	0.38	0.38	0.43	0.41
School ICC	0.03	0.04	0.09	0.04
Year-within-school ICC	0.21	0.14	0.17	0.12
Residual (teacher-level) ICC	0.76	0.83	0.74	0.84
School reliability	0.19	0.33	0.45	0.34

Table B.4
Average Number of Teacher Respondents per School, Combined Across Years

Scale	Site			
	HCPS	PPS	SCS	Aspire
Supportive district climate	17.63	41.76	19.02	29.28
Supportive and respectful school environment	17.46	41.24	18.79	28.95
Impetus for and impact of PD	17.58	41.44	18.92	29.08
Alignment and relevance of PD	17.58	41.63	18.99	29.05
Rapport among teachers	17.74	41.94	19.20	29.33
Expectations for students	13.09	31.57	13.80	21.40
Support for the evaluation system	16.76	32.78	18.19	27.68
Quality of the observation process	16.94	31.76	18.41	28.05
Validity of the student achievement component of the evaluation system	9.98	15.13	8.15	13.43
Validity of the student input component of the evaluation system	3.87	26.94	15.39	24.58
Opinions about the evaluation system (negative)	12.80	24.17	14.01	20.70
Fairness of compensation	13.32	30.70	14.52	21.75

cator for whether the school was a middle school), and r_i is a random error associated with the school. In this model, the parameter of primary interest is β_1, which represents the change in the mature-implementation VAM score for a one-unit increase in the school scale value.

We conducted a separate regression for each of the 12 scales in each of the four sites, for a total of 48 regressions, and then conducted a meta-analysis for each scale combining across the sites to produce an additional 12 results. Given such a large number of significance tests, readers should keep in mind that some of the significant effects we identified could have been significant by chance. We did not make any adjustments for multiple comparisons.

Descriptive Statistics on the Outcome Variable and the Covariates for the Sample of Schools Included in the Survey Scale Analysis

Table B.5 shows descriptive statistics for the outcome variable and the covariates.

Table B.5
Means and Standard Deviations of the Outcome Variable and the Covariates for the Sample of Schools Included in the Analysis

	Site			
	HCPS	**PPS**	**SCS**	**Aspire**
Variable	**Mean (SD)**	**Mean (SD)**	**Mean (SD)**	**Mean (SD)**
Outcome variable				
VAM score, mature-implementation period	0.04 (0.91)	0.01 (0.44)	0.00 (0.59)	0.01 (0.17)
Covariates				
VAM score, baseline period	0.02 (0.75)	0.01 (0.52)	0.00 (0.72)	0.01 (0.22)
Percentage of ELLs	10.32 (8.31)	3.27 (7.09)	7.39 (11.31)	27.25 (20.35)
Percentage of students with disabilities	20.28 (4.01)	13.69 (4.83)	1.88 (1.09)	8.22 (1.66)
Percentage of LIM students	54.61 (27.00)	44.15 (20.53)	87.52 (15.79)	68.01 (29.45)
Percentage of middle schools in the analysis	22.40 (41.81)	23.25 (42.75)	24.62 (43.24)	28.57 (46.29)
Number of schools	183	43	130	21

NOTES: All of the school demographic variables are from the mature-implementation period. We elected to include the mature-implementation measures because, in theory, the preinitiative period VAM score should account for demographic characteristics during the preinitiative period. VAM scores are standardized for each site and then shrunken using empirical Bayes techniques to reflect the precision of each school-level average. This shrinkage leads to standard deviations of less than one, with greater shrinkage occurring in smaller sites. See the note to Table A.2 for more information. SD = standard deviation.

How to Read the Meta-Analysis Figures

Figures B.1 through B.12 were created using the meta-analysis procedure (conducted in Stata, using the *metan* command). The following is a guide to how to read them:

- For each site, the horizontal black line shows the 95-percent confidence interval (CI) for the effect of the scale on the outcome, and the black dot in the middle of the line indicates the point estimate. If the horizontal line does not intersect with the vertical black line at zero (i.e., if the CI does not include zero), the effect is significant at $p < 0.05$ based on a z-test.
- The numerical values of the point estimate (i.e., the estimated effect size) and the endpoints of the CI are listed under the "Estimated effect size (95% CI)" heading. The point estimate is the same as the number in the corresponding cell of Table 3.3.
- For all 12 figures, we have set the horizontal axis range to run from −4 to +4 effect size units (i.e., standard deviations of the mature-implementation VAM score). For nearly all of the scales, this range was sufficient to capture the full width of each CI.
- The number in the "Weight (%)" column is the percentage of the total weight that each site was given in the meta-analysis. Each site's weight is a function of the precision of the site's estimate of the mean; sites that have smaller standard errors (smaller CIs) are given more weight.
- The dotted vertical red line is the point estimate for the meta-analysis, and the horizontal width of the large blue diamond is the 95-percent CI for the meta-analysis point estimate. If the diamond does not intersect with the vertical black line at zero, the overall effect is significant at $p < 0.05$. As with the individual sites, the numerical values of the point estimate and the endpoints of the CI also are shown.

- If the black horizontal line for any given site does not cross the vertical dotted red line, the effect for that site is significantly different (at $p < 0.05$) from the overall effect.
- The *I*-squared results next to the "Overall" label indicate whether there was significant variation across sites in the effect. The percentage is the percentage of the observed variation across sites that is true, and the p-value indicates whether the variation across sites was significantly different from zero (i.e., no variance across sites).
- As indicated by the figure notes, the meta-analysis treats the study-specific error component as random effects (i.e., as drawn from a population of studies), as is conventional in meta-analyses (DerSimonian and Laird, 2015). The precision of the overall mean is a function of both the standard error of the estimated effect for each site and the variance in effects among the sites.

Figure B.1
Meta-Analysis Results, Supportive District Climate

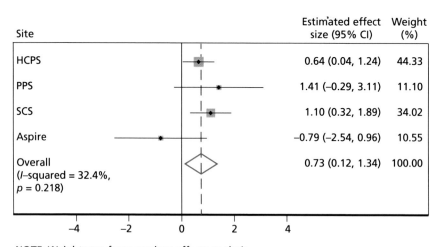

NOTE: Weights are from random effects analysis.

Figure B.2
Meta-Analysis Results, Supportive and Respectful School Environment

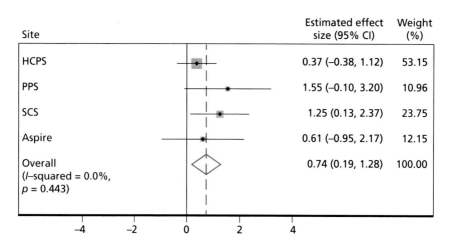

Site	Estimated effect size (95% CI)	Weight (%)
HCPS	0.48 (−0.11, 1.07)	32.31
PPS	0.48 (−0.39, 1.36)	14.62
SCS	0.75 (−0.19, 1.68)	12.87
Aspire	0.05 (−0.48, 0.58)	40.19
Overall (I–squared = 0.0%, p = 0.535)	0.34 (0.01, 0.68)	100.00

NOTE: Weights are from random effects analysis.

Figure B.3
Meta-Analysis Results, Impetus for and Impact of Professional Development

Site	Estimated effect size (95% CI)	Weight (%)
HCPS	0.37 (−0.38, 1.12)	53.15
PPS	1.55 (−0.10, 3.20)	10.96
SCS	1.25 (0.13, 2.37)	23.75
Aspire	0.61 (−0.95, 2.17)	12.15
Overall (I–squared = 0.0%, p = 0.443)	0.74 (0.19, 1.28)	100.00

NOTE: Weights are from random effects analysis.

Figure B.4
Meta-Analysis Results, Alignment and Relevance of Professional Development

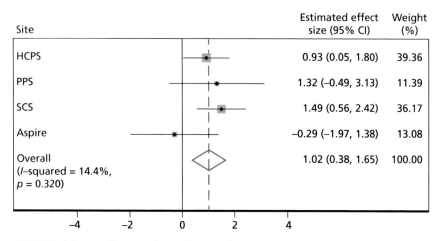

NOTE: Weights are from random effects analysis.

Figure B.5
Meta-Analysis Results, Rapport Among Teachers

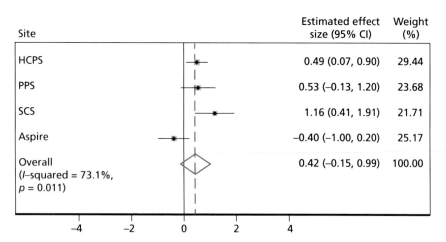

NOTE: Weights are from random effects analysis.

Figure B.6
Meta-Analysis Results, Expectations for Students

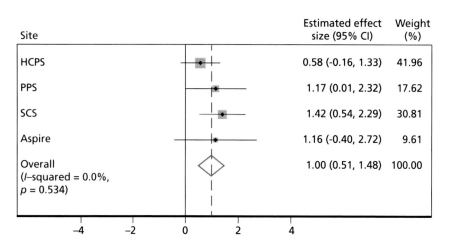

Site	Estimated effect size (95% CI)	Weight (%)
HCPS	−0.03 (−0.58, 0.52)	28.94
PPS	−0.47 (−1.37, 0.44)	21.46
SCS	1.36 (0.42, 2.30)	20.83
Aspire	0.64 (0.08, 1.19)	28.76
Overall (I-squared = 71.3%, p = 0.015)	0.36 (−0.30, 1.02)	100.00

NOTE: Weights are from random effects analysis.

Figure B.7
Meta-Analysis Results, Support for the Evaluation System

Site	Estimated effect size (95% CI)	Weight (%)
HCPS	0.58 (-0.16, 1.33)	41.96
PPS	1.17 (0.01, 2.32)	17.62
SCS	1.42 (0.54, 2.29)	30.81
Aspire	1.16 (-0.40, 2.72)	9.61
Overall (I-squared = 0.0%, p = 0.534)	1.00 (0.51, 1.48)	100.00

NOTE: Weights are from random effects analysis.

Figure B.8
Meta-Analysis Results, Quality of the Observation Process

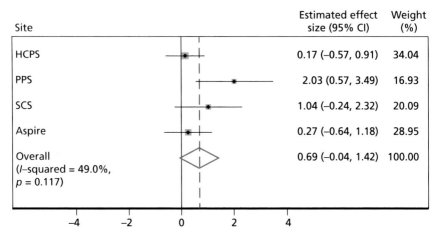

NOTE: Weights are from random effects analysis.

Figure B.9
Meta-Analysis Results, Validity of the Student Achievement Component of the Evaluation System

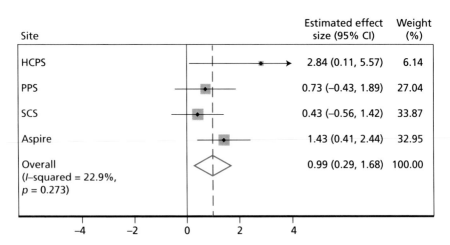

NOTE: Weights are from random effects analysis.

Figure B.10
Meta-Analysis Results, Validity of the Student Input Component of the Evaluation System

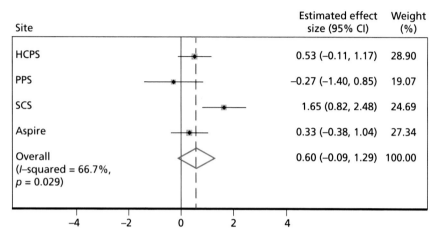

Site		Estimated effect size (95% CI)	Weight (%)
HCPS		0.53 (−0.11, 1.17)	28.90
PPS		−0.27 (−1.40, 0.85)	19.07
SCS		1.65 (0.82, 2.48)	24.69
Aspire		0.33 (−0.38, 1.04)	27.34
Overall (*I*–squared = 66.7%, *p* = 0.029)		0.60 (−0.09, 1.29)	100.00

NOTE: Weights are from random effects analysis.

Figure B.11
Meta-Analysis Results, Opinions About the Evaluation System (Negative)

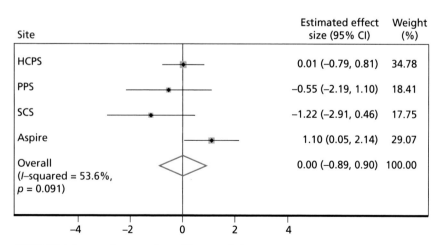

Site		Estimated effect size (95% CI)	Weight (%)
HCPS		0.01 (−0.79, 0.81)	34.78
PPS		−0.55 (−2.19, 1.10)	18.41
SCS		−1.22 (−2.91, 0.46)	17.75
Aspire		1.10 (0.05, 2.14)	29.07
Overall (*I*–squared = 53.6%, *p* = 0.091)		0.00 (−0.89, 0.90)	100.00

NOTE: Weights are from random effects analysis.

Figure B.12
Meta-Analysis Results, Fairness of Compensation

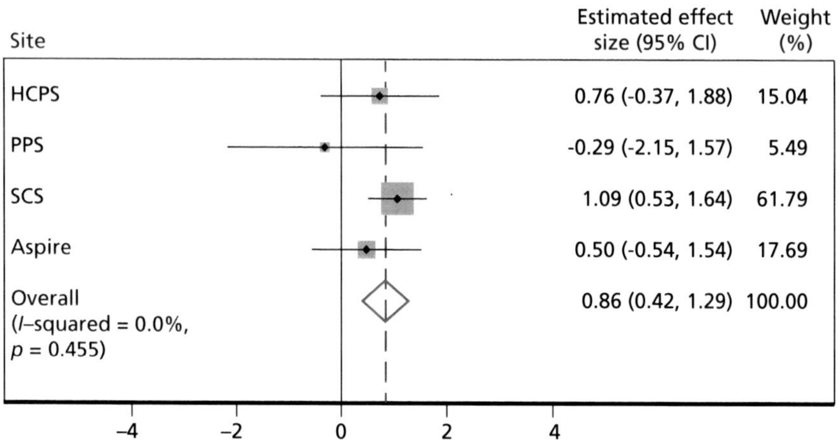

NOTE: Weights are from random effects analysis.

Pairwise Correlations of School-Level Scale Values, All Sites Combined and in Each Site

In Table B.6, we present correlations among the scale variables at the school level for all sites combined. Tables B.7, B.8, B.9, and B.10 show the pairwise correlations of the scale variables within each of the four sites.

Table B.6
Correlations Among the Scale Variables, at the School Level, All Sites Combined

Variable	Supportive District Climate	Supportive and Respectful School Environment[a]	Impetus for and Impact of PD	Alignment and Relevance of PD[a]	Rapport Among Teachers	Expectations for Students	Support for the Evaluation System	Quality of the Observation Process	Validity of the Student Achievement Component	Validity of the Student Input Component	Opinions About the Evaluation System (Negative)	Fairness of Compensation
Supportive district climate[a]	1.00											
Supportive and respectful school environment[a]	0.48	1.00										
Impetus for and impact of PD	0.49	0.33	1.00									
Alignment and relevance of PD[a]	0.56	0.48	0.67	1.00								
Rapport among teachers[a]	0.32	0.44	0.07	0.28	1.00							
Expectations for students[a]	0.26	0.21	0.10	0.21	0.32	1.00						
Support for the evaluation system[a]	0.68	0.48	0.49	0.51	0.18	0.19	1.00					

Table B.6—Continued

Variable	Supportive District Climate	Supportive and Respectful School Environment	Impetus for and Impact of PD	Alignment and Relevance of PD	Rapport Among Teachers	Expectations for Students	Support for the Evaluation System	Quality of the Observation Process	Validity of the Student Achievement Component	Validity of the Student Input Component	Opinions About the Evaluation System (Negative)	Fairness of Compensation
Quality of the observation process[a]	0.59	0.57	0.46	0.50	0.23	0.11	0.73	1.00				
Validity of the student achievement component of the evaluation system[b]	0.24	0.12	0.24	0.26	0.01	0.05	0.28	0.17	1.00			
Validity of the student input component of the evaluation system[c]	0.27	0.14	0.22	0.20	0.00	0.18	0.34	0.13	0.16	1.00		
Opinions about the evaluation system (negative)[b]	-0.35	-0.25	-0.19	-0.25	0.00	-0.03	-0.40	-0.31	-0.09	-0.20	1.00	

Table B.6—Continued

Variable	Supportive District Climate	Supportive and Respectful School Environment	Impetus for and Impact of PD	Alignment and Relevance of PD	Rapport Among Teachers	Expectations for Students	Support for the Evaluation System	Quality of the Observation Process	Validity of the Student Achievement Component	Validity of the Student Input Component	Opinions About the Evaluation System (Negative)	Fairness of Compensation
Fairness of compensation[b]	0.43	0.18	0.30	0.26	0.01	0.05	0.41	0.26	0.29	0.22	−0.17	1.00

NOTE: N/A = not applicable.

[a] For all cells in this row, $N = 377$.

[b] For all cells in this row, $N = 370$.

[c] For all cells in this row, $N = 366$.

Table B.7
Correlations Among the Scale Variables, at the School Level, HCPS

Variable	Supportive District Climate	Supportive and Respectful School Environment	Impetus for and Impact of PD	Alignment and Relevance of PD	Rapport Among Teachers	Expectations for Students	Support for the Evaluation System	Quality of the Observation Process	Validity of the Student Achievement Component	Validity of the Student Input Component	Opinions About the Evaluation System (Negative)	Fairness of Compensation
Supportive district climate[a]	1.00											
Supportive and respectful school environment[a]	0.50	1.00										
Impetus for and impact of PD[a]	0.43	0.28	1.00									
Alignment and relevance of PD[a]	0.59	0.49	0.67	1.00								
Rapport among teachers[a]	0.41	0.48	0.02	0.27	1.00							
Expectations for students[a]	0.28	0.21	0.05	0.17	0.34	1.00						

Table B.7—Continued

Variable	Supportive District Climate	Supportive and Respectful School Environment	Impetus for and Impact of PD	Alignment and Relevance of PD	Rapport Among Teachers	Expectations for Students	Support for the Evaluation System	Quality of the Observation Process	Validity of the Student Achievement Component	Validity of the Student Input Component	Opinions About the Evaluation System (Negative)	Fairness of Compensation
Support for the evaluation system[a]	0.70	0.46	0.49	0.56	0.21	0.18	1.00					
Quality of the observation process[a]	0.65	0.52	0.48	0.53	0.16	0.11	0.82	1.00				
Validity of the student achievement component of the evaluation system[a]	0.31	0.35	0.33	0.40	0.12	0.07	0.36	0.28	1.00			
Validity of the student input component of the evaluation system[b]	0.18	0.11	0.07	0.06	0.02	0.23	0.28	0.15	0.16	1.00		

Table B.7—Continued

Variable	Supportive District Climate	Supportive and Respectful School Environment	Impetus for and Impact of PD	Alignment and Relevance of PD	Rapport Among Teachers	Expectations for Students	Support for the Evaluation System	Quality of the Observation Process	Validity of the Student Achievement Component	Validity of the Student Input Component	Opinions About the Evaluation System (Negative)	Fairness of Compensation
Opinions about the evaluation system (negative)[a]	-0.32	-0.27	-0.20	-0.21	0.06	-0.04	-0.41	-0.33	-0.18	-0.18	1.00	
Fairness of compensation[a]	0.40	0.22	0.23	0.36	0.11	0.06	0.47	0.37	0.24	0.09	-0.21	1.00

NOTE: N/A = not applicable.

[a] For all cells in this row, N = 183.

[b] For all cells in this row, N = 172.

Table B.8
Correlations Among the Scale Variables, at the School Level, PPS

Variable	Supportive District Climate	Supportive and Respectful School Environment	Impetus for and Impact of PD	Alignment and Relevance of PD	Rapport Among Teachers	Expectations for Students	Support for the Evaluation System	Quality of the Observation Process	Validity of the Student Achievement Component	Validity of the Student Input Component	Opinions About the Evaluation System (Negative)	Fairness of Compensation
Supportive district climate	1.00											
Supportive and respectful school environment	0.63	1.00										
Impetus for and impact of PD	0.50	0.32	1.00									
Alignment and relevance of PD	0.53	0.48	0.73	1.00								
Rapport among teachers	0.46	0.39	0.14	0.25	1.00							
Expectations for students	0.31	0.17	0.20	0.36	0.32	1.00						

Table B.8—Continued

Variable	Supportive District Climate	Supportive and Respectful School Environment	Impetus for and Impact of PD	Alignment and Relevance of PD	Rapport Among Teachers	Expectations for Students	Support for the Evaluation System	Quality of the Observation Process	Validity of the Student Achievement Component	Validity of the Student Input Component	Opinions About the Evaluation System (Negative)	Fairness of Compensation
Support for the evaluation system	0.77	0.62	0.53	0.48	0.28	0.20	1.00					
Quality of the observation process	0.55	0.55	0.34	0.33	0.28	-0.13	0.63	1.00				
Validity of the student achievement component of the evaluation system	0.05	-0.01	0.30	0.21	-0.01	0.02	0.04	0.15	1.00			
Validity of the student input component of the evaluation system	0.36	0.20	0.40	0.42	0.14	0.38	0.48	-0.05	-0.17	1.00		

Table B.8—Continued

Variable	Supportive District Climate	Supportive and Respectful School Environment	Impetus for and Impact of PD	Alignment and Relevance of PD	Rapport Among Teachers	Expectations for Students	Support for the Evaluation System	Quality of the Observation Process	Validity of the Student Achievement Component	Validity of the Student Input Component	Opinions About the Evaluation System (Negative)	Fairness of Compensation
Opinions about the evaluation system (negative)	-0.39	-0.35	-0.20	-0.36	-0.36	-0.21	-0.44	-0.32	-0.06	-0.10	1.00	
Fairness of compensation	0.20	0.14	0.20	0.09	0.13	-0.10	0.08	0.01	0.08	0.13	-0.08	1.00

NOTES: $N = 43$ for all cells in this table. N/A = not applicable.

Table B.9
Correlations Among the Scale Variables, at the School Level, SCS

Variable	Supportive District Climate	Supportive and Respectful School Environment	Impetus for and Impact of PD	Alignment and Relevance of PD	Rapport Among Teachers	Expectations for Students	Support for the Evaluation System	Quality of the Observation Process	Validity of the Student Achievement Component	Validity of the Student Input Component	Opinions About the Evaluation System (Negative)	Fairness of Compensation
Supportive district climate[a]	1.00											
Supportive and respectful school environment[a]	0.45	1.00										
Impetus for and impact of PD[a]	0.59	0.40	1.00									
Alignment and relevance of PD[a]	0.53	0.51	0.67	1.00								
Rapport among teachers[a]	0.13	0.40	0.09	0.30	1.00							
Expectations for students[a]	0.26	0.26	0.22	0.30	0.17	1.00						

Table B.9—Continued

Variable	Supportive District Climate	Supportive and Respectful School Environment	Impetus for and Impact of PD	Alignment and Relevance of PD	Rapport Among Teachers	Expectations for Students	Support for the Evaluation System	Quality of the Observation Process	Validity of the Student Achievement Component	Validity of the Student Input Component	Opinions About the Evaluation System (Negative)	Fairness of Compensation
Support for the evaluation system[a]	0.68	0.50	0.48	0.48	0.12	0.28	1.00					
Quality of the observation process[a]	0.53	0.65	0.45	0.57	0.37	0.21	0.69	1.00				
Validity of the student achievement component of the evaluation system[b]	0.37	0.15	0.28	0.29	-0.03	0.07	0.42	0.27	1.00			
Validity of the student input component of the evaluation system[a]	0.42	0.18	0.39	0.31	0.00	0.25	0.42	0.21	0.41	1.00		

Table B.9—Continued

Variable	Supportive District Climate	Supportive and Respectful School Environment	Impetus for and Impact of PD	Alignment and Relevance of PD	Rapport Among Teachers	Expectations for Students	Support for the Evaluation System	Quality of the Observation Process	Validity of the Student Achievement Component	Validity of the Student Input Component	Opinions About the Evaluation System (Negative)	Fairness of Compensation
Opinions about the evaluation system (negative)[b]	-0.46	-0.27	-0.22	-0.39	0.04	-0.04	-0.48	-0.36	-0.23	-0.29	1.00	
Fairness of compensation[b]	0.56	0.23	0.46	0.27	-0.09	0.11	0.49	0.30	0.35	0.39	-0.26	1.00

NOTE: N/A = not applicable.

[a] For all cells in this row, N = 130.

[b] For all cells in this row, N = 123.

Table B.10
Correlations Among the Scale Variables, at the School Level, Aspire

Variable	Supportive District Climate	Supportive and Respectful School Environment	Impetus for and Impact of PD	Alignment and Relevance of PD	Rapport Among Teachers	Expectations for Students	Support for the Evaluation System	Quality of the Observation Process	Validity of the Student Achievement Component	Validity of the Student Input Component	Opinions About the Evaluation System (Negative)	Fairness of Compensation
Supportive district climate	1.00											
Supportive and respectful school environment	0.75	1.00										
Impetus for and impact of PD	0.59	0.78	1.00									
Alignment and relevance of PD	0.57	0.67	0.84	1.00								
Rapport among teachers	0.68	0.43	0.55	0.65	1.00							
Expectations for students	0.32	0.22	0.28	0.33	0.56	1.00						

Table B.10—Continued

Variable	Supportive District Climate	Supportive and Respectful School Environment	Impetus for and Impact of PD	Alignment and Relevance of PD	Rapport Among Teachers	Expectations for Students	Support for the Evaluation System	Quality of the Observation Process	Validity of the Student Achievement Component	Validity of the Student Input Component	Opinions About the Evaluation System (Negative)	Fairness of Compensation
Support for the evaluation system	0.36	0.45	0.46	0.27	0.19	0.23	1.00					
Quality of the observation process	0.60	0.74	0.52	0.41	0.25	0.26	0.72	1.00				
Validity of the student achievement component of the evaluation system	-0.18	0.08	0.20	0.09	0.04	0.30	0.21	-0.10	1.00			
Validity of the student input component of the evaluation system	0.02	0.10	0.25	0.03	-0.28	-0.29	0.12	0.07	-0.24	1.00		

Table B.10—Continued

Variable	Supportive District Climate	Supportive and Respectful School Environment	Impetus for and Impact of PD	Alignment and Relevance of PD	Rapport Among Teachers	Expectations for Students	Support for the Evaluation System	Quality of the Observation Process	Validity of the Student Achievement Component	Validity of the Student Input Component	Opinions About the Evaluation System (Negative)	Fairness of Compensation
Opinions about the evaluation system (negative)	-0.16	-0.01	0.16	0.28	0.12	0.47	0.05	0.00	0.55	-0.31	1.00	
Fairness of compensation	0.08	0.28	0.17	-0.03	-0.03	0.08	0.55	0.40	0.28	-0.25	-0.09	1.00

NOTES: $N = 21$ for all cells in this table. N/A = not applicable.

References

Ascher, Carol, and Cindy Maguire, *Beating the Odds: How Thirteen NYC Schools Bring Low-Performing Ninth-Graders to Timely Graduation and College Enrollment*, Providence, R.I.: Annenberg Institute for School Reform, 2007.

Baird, Matthew D., John Engberg, Gerald Paul Hunter, and Benjamin Master, *Improving Teaching Effectiveness: Access to Effective Teaching—The Intensive Partnerships for Effective Teaching Through 2013–2014*, Santa Monica, Calif.: RAND Corporation, RR-1295/4-BMGF, 2016. As of April 6, 2020: https://www.rand.org/pubs/research_reports/RR1295z4.html

Bush-Mecenas, Susan, and Julie A. Marsh, "The DIVE Approach: Using Case-Ordered Meta-Matrices and Theory-Based Data Displays to Analyze Multiple Case Study Data," in Chad R. Lochmiller, ed., *Complementary Research Methods for Educational Leadership and Policy Studies*, Cham, Switzerland: Palgrave Macmillan, 2018, pp. 33–56.

DerSimonian, Rebecca, and Nan Laird, "Meta-Analysis in Clinical Trials Revisited," *Contemporary Clinical Trials*, Vol. 45, 2015, pp. 139–145.

Dobbie, Will, and Roland G. Fryer, Jr., "Getting Beneath the Veil of Effective Schools: Evidence from New York City," *American Economic Journal: Applied Economics*, Vol. 5, No. 4, 2013, pp. 28–60.

Garet, Michael S., Deborah J. Holtzman, Brian M. Stecher, and John Engberg, *Improving Teaching Effectiveness: The Intensive Partnerships for Effective Teaching Through 2015–2016—Addendum*, Santa Monica, Calif.: RAND Corporation, RR-2242/2-BMGF, 2019. As of March 5, 2020: https://www.rand.org/pubs/research_reports/RR2242.html

Kraft, Matthew A., William H. Marinell, and Darrick Shen-Wei Yee, "School Organizational Contexts, Teacher Turnover, and Student Achievement: Evidence from Panel Data," *American Educational Research Journal*, Vol. 53, No. 5, 2016, pp. 1411–1449.

Langer, Judith A., "Beating the Odds: Teaching Middle and High School Students to Read and Write Well," *American Educational Research Journal*, Vol. 38, No. 4, 2001, pp. 837–880.

Leithwood, Kenneth, and Blair Mascall, "Collective Leadership Effects on Student Achievement," *Educational Administration Quarterly*, Vol. 44, No. 4, 2008, pp. 529–561.

Marzano, Robert J., Timothy Waters, and Brian A. McNulty, *School Leadership That Works: From Research to Results*, Alexandria, Va.: Association for Supervision and Curriculum Development, 2001.

Stecher, Brian M., Deborah J. Holtzman, Michael S. Garet, Laura S. Hamilton, John Engberg, Elizabeth D. Steiner, Abby Robyn, Matthew D. Baird, Italo A. Gutierrez, Evan D. Peet, Iliana Brodziak de los Reyes, Kaitlin Fronberg, Gabriel Weinberger, Gerald Paul Hunter, and Jay Chambers, *Improving Teaching Effectiveness: Final Report—The Intensive Partnerships for Effective Teaching Through 2015–2016*, Santa Monica, Calif.: RAND Corporation, RR-2242-BMGF, 2018. As of March 5, 2020:
https://www.rand.org/pubs/research_reports/RR2242.html

Wahlstrom, Kyla L., Karen Seashore Louis, Kenneth Leithwood, and Stephen E. Anderson, *Investigating the Links to Improved Student Learning: Executive Summary of Research Findings*, New York: The Wallace Foundation, 2010. As of March 5, 2020:
https://www.wallacefoundation.org/knowledge-center/Documents/Investigating-the-Links-to-Improved-Student-Learning-Executive-Summary.pdf